D1581388

The Gothic: 250 Years of Success

Your Guide to Gothic Literature and Culture

A J Blakemont

Published by Dark Romantic Worlds, 2014 (updated in 2016)
42 Philbeach House
Dale, Pembrokeshire
SA62 3QU
United Kingdom

Stock images were purchased from 123RF.com and canstockphoto.com

ISBN: 1502965682
ISBN-13: 978-1502965684

CONTENTS

The Gothic: 250 Years of Success   1

Part 1: From Ancient Fears to Modern Aesthetics   7

     Chapter 1.1: A Bit of History   7

     Chapter 1.2: Gothic Revival   11

     Chapter 1.3: Sublime Terrors, or the Aesthetics of the Dark   15

     Chapter 1.4: The Gothic as a Literary Style   18

     Chapter 1.5: The Gothic in Visual Arts   21

     Chapter 1.6: The Gothic in Modern Music   29

Part 2: Gothic Evolution   35

     Chapter 2.1: Evolutionary Tree of the Gothic   35

     Chapter 2.2: Gothic Fantasy   42

     Chapter 2.3: Gothic Romance   47

     Chapter 2.4: Gothic Horror   51

     Chapter 2.5: Women's Rights and Female Gothic   59

     Chapter 2.6: Gothic Themes and Motifs   61

Part 3: Underground versus Mainstream: Antagonism… or Synergy?   69

     Chapter 3.1: Cinema and Television Series   69

     Chapter 3.2: Gothic Influences on Metal Music and Alternative Rock   72

     Chapter 3.3: Fashion   74

     Chapter 3.4: Games   76

     Chapter 3.5: Digital Art, Internet and Social Media   78

     Chapter 3.6: Gothic Subcultures and Global Tribes   79

Epilogue: Many Happy Returns!   84

Further Reading   88

Index   90

Moret, *La mode illustrée, Journal de la famille,* 1887

The Gothic: 250 Years of Success

In December 1764 appeared a curious book titled *The Castle of Otranto*. Its preface stated:

> The following work was found in the library of an ancient Catholic family in the north of England. It was printed at Naples, in the black letter, in the year 1529. How much sooner it was written does not appear. The principal incidents are such as were believed in the darkest ages of Christianity; but the language and conduct have nothing that savours of barbarism.

The preface went on to speculate that this story had been written during the Crusades, between 1095 and 1243. A haunted castle, a mysterious prophecy, an evil and manipulative aristocrat, two young and beautiful heroines, a forbidden love and lots of action – such are the ingredients of this wildly imaginative melodrama.

Despite an initially positive critical reception, this unlikely story could have remained a footnote in the history of literature, as did other literary curiosities. However, the following year, a second edition of this book was published, and, this time, its true nature was revealed by the author. *The Castle of Otranto: A Gothic Story* was a work of fiction written by Horace Walpole, a forty-eight-year-old English aristocrat known for his passion for the medieval period and Gothic architecture.

In this stylish, rationalist 18th century, dominated by the baroque and the Classicism, Walpole was viewed as an eccentric. He went as far as to transform his villa at Strawberry Hill (just outside London) into an imitation of a Gothic castle. In the preface to the second edition of *The Castle of Otranto*, Walpole explained that his book was "an attempt to blend the two kinds of romance, the ancient and the modern". In other words, he transposed his love for medieval art into literature and thus created the first neo-Gothic fictional work in history.

In the 1760s, the world was not yet ready for the onslaught of the Gothic. However, two decades later, England was ready, as were other European countries that went through radical social changes.

The Gothic novel exploded in the 1790s and the 1800s, when, in England, up to 20 per cent of all published titles belonged to this type of literature. Paradoxically, the effects of this cultural phenomenon were as profound as the books that caused it were shallow. Few Gothic novels published in the 18th century had literary merit (those by Ann Radcliffe being among the rare exceptions). More than their intrinsic quality, it was their ability to excite the imagination of a broad readership that made them so influential. The 18th-century Gothic fiction was probably the first popular genre in the history of Western civilization; it was the prototype of what we call a genre nowadays.

The success of this early wave of terrifying novels was short-lived, and, in the 1820s, readers grew tired of this kind of story. Nevertheless, 19th-century literature would not be the same without the spark of wild imagination brought by the Gothic novel. This genre created a portal between the mysterious past and the rational present through which the power of medieval fancy could relive to inseminate the modern culture. It inspired Jane Austen to write her first novel, *Northanger Abbey*, a satirical, yet respectful parody of the Radcliffean Gothic. It influenced Walter Scott, the father of historical fiction. It paved the road for the budding Romantic Movement, in particular its darker forms, and we can see its imprint in Byron's poems or in Mary Shelley's *Frankenstein*.

Some literary critics viewed the Gothic as biologists view extinct species, like a relic of the past, something that had a role in evolution, but was now history. As a *genre* the Gothic is no more; nevertheless, as an *artistic style* it is as strong nowadays as it was two centuries ago. It was its ability to evolve beyond the boundaries of a genre that made it so influential and widespread. By the first decade of the 19th century, the Gothic had invaded literature and, to a lesser extent, theatrical drama and visual arts. By the first decade of the 21st century, the Gothic was everywhere: cinema, TV, comic books, music, internet, role-playing games (RPGs), video games, digital art, and fashion. Not only was it adopted by every form of art and every media, but it also penetrated most genres; we can find its influence in fantasy, science fiction (SF), thrillers, romance, historical fiction, and literary fiction.

What is the Gothic?

Despite the number of studies devoted to this subject, the precise definition of the Gothic remains as elusive as the creatures that haunt the Castle of Otranto. The Gothic has been associated with such different things as horror fiction, romance, feminism, the uncanny, post-punk, metal music, and even Satanism.

To give a simple answer to a complex question, let's say that the Gothic is a particular approach to artistic creation, a set of aesthetic values. Contrary to a common misconception, the Gothic does not have to be frightening; it is not synonymous with horror. It can also be funny, satirical or full of self-derision. Sometimes, it can also be deep and thought-provoking. A story about ghosts, vampires or demons may be Gothic or not. Conversely, a Gothic story does not necessarily involve the supernatural. It is the *mood* that defines the Gothic, not the plot or the setting. It is not about monsters and castles; it is about the atmosphere created and the emotions evoked. It is about the weird, the paradoxical, the anti-conventional, the surreal.

On a deeper level, one might say that the Gothic is an art of subversion. In their *A Short History of Fantasy* (2009), Farah Mendlesohn and Edward James write: "The very idea of a world that could be controlled and understood was subverted into a mode of literature, the Gothic, in which this surface world is a delusion." The most common motif in Gothic fiction is the crossing of the boundaries: boundaries between the past and the present, the real and the imaginary, the natural and the unnatural (or the artificial), the human and the animal, and even between life and death.

Two Centuries of Success

Some critics argue that the Gothic is an episodic phenomenon emerging at a time of social change, and it is undeniable that Gothic narratives reflect the anxieties of their time. However, one might look at the history of this mode of fiction-making as a story of continuous success. During the last two centuries, every generation had its own form of

Gothic fiction.

In the first decades of the 19th century, when the original Gothic genre was losing momentum, its place was rapidly filled by dark Romanticism. Among the most prolific writers of that period, we can mention the German E T A Hoffmann and the French Théophile Gautier. In the 1830s and 1840s, dark Romanticism reached its full creative potential with writers such as Edgar Allan Poe, Nathaniel Hawthorne and Herman Melville, who were among the most influential American authors of the 19th century. The publication of *Les Fleurs du mal* (*The Flowers of Evil*, 1857) by the French poet Charles Baudelaire opened the way for new and highly innovative artistic movements, in particular Symbolism and Surrealism.

The Victorian Gothic is well known thanks to the literary masterpieces such as *Strange Case of Dr Jekyll and Mr Hyde* by Robert Louis Stevenson (1886), *The Picture of Dorian Gray* by Oscar Wilde (1890), and Bram Stoker's *Dracula* (1897). The pioneers of SF Jules Verne and H G Wells also drew inspiration from the Gothic fiction (*The Carpathian Castle*, 1892; *The Island of Doctor Moreau*, 1896).

In the 1910s and 1920s, it was the turn of filmmakers to tap into the Gothic, German Expressionism giving a new image to the old monsters in *Nosferatu* (F W Murnau, 1922) and *Metropolis* (Fritz Lang, 1927) – discussed in Chapter 1.5. The 1930s witnessed the golden age of the black-and-white monster film, the most noteworthy movies being *Dracula* (Tod Browning, 1931) starring Bela Lugosi, *Frankenstein* (James Whale, 1931) starring Boris Karloff, *The Mummy* (Karl Freund, 1932), and *King Kong* (Merian C Cooper and Ernest B Schoedsack, 1933).

During the Second World War, the Gothic made its way to the pages of comic books, a new, yet hugely popular form of artistic expression. Indeed, several fictional universes developed by comic book authors are distinctly Gothic, starting with Batman, a vigilante fighting crime in a metropolis meaningfully called Gotham City.

In the 1950s and 1960s, the Gothic was overshadowed by cultural phenomena such as rock and roll and the emergence of the so-called pop music. This period of economic recovery was marked by an atmosphere of optimism (at least in the countries that won the war) and, at first glance, was not prone to adopt the dark culture as a popular form of fiction. However, the Gothic was still there, doing what it does best

– hiding in the maze of underground cultures, waiting for its hour to make its triumphant return.

This return happened progressively, starting in the 1970s and culminating in the 2000s. This impressive counterattack of the "dark side" operated on several fronts. In 1974 appeared the first novel by Stephen King, *Carrie,* and two years later Anne Rice published the first tome of her influential series *The Vampire Chronicles (Interview with the Vampire,* 1976). In music, post-punk bands such as Bauhaus and Joy Division launched what will later be called Goth rock. The 70s and early 80s were a period of frantic creativity and experimentation, and this experimentation generated not only new musical genres, but entire subcultures revolving around those genres (discussed in Chapters 1.6 and 3.6).

During that period, the film industry went through its own revolution. The development of special effects techniques created a cultural phenomenon: the blockbuster. The first *Star Wars* (George Lucas, 1977) launched one of the most profitable franchises in the history of cinema. In *Alien* (1979), Ridley Scott created a shocking, futuristic aesthetic of fear. *Blade Runner* (Ridley Scott, 1982) was less successful from a commercial point of view, but was influential from a cultural perspective.

Cyberpunk, a Gothic SF subgenre, was born in the 80s, William Gibson being the most well-known writer associated with it. The popularity of this subgenre reached its peak with the release of *The Matrix* (Wachowski Brothers) in 1999.

In the 2000s, the Gothic reached an unprecedented level of popularity. This event can be compared with a perfect storm, several causes coinciding to amplify its effect (discussed in Part 3 of this book). One of those causes was the development of digital art as it opened the gates on a new world of creativity. The website DeviantArt launched in 2000 allowed thousands of photographers and artists to display their work online. Internet and social media promoted the creation of virtual communities around particular areas of interest, Gothic subcultures being among them.

Television was traditionally more resistant to the influence of the Gothic than other media; however, when TV did draw from the Gothic tradition, the result was noteworthy. *X-Files,* for example, was among the most popular TV series in the 1990s. We can also mention *The Twilight Zone* (1959-64 for the original series), *Dark Shadows* (1966-1971),

Tales from the Crypt (1989-96), *Six Feet Under* (2001-05), *Dead Like Me* (2003-04), *True Blood* (2008-14), and *Penny Dreadful* (2014-16).

After 250 years, not only is the Gothic alive and well, but it is thriving, constantly reinventing and rejuvenating itself. It has proved to be one of the most fertile artistic traditions in the history of modern civilization; its ability to crossbreed with other cultures to take on new forms seems boundless. The Gothic became a global phenomenon, and we can find it from South America to Japan.

The purpose of the present book is not to discuss in detail every work influenced by the Gothic; such endeavor would call for several volumes (most likely several dozens of them). Its objective is to provide an overview of the Gothic culture in all its diversity. Part 1 addresses the following questions: what is the Gothic, how it came to be and how it works. Part 2 discusses how the Gothic fiction evolved over the last 250 years. Part 3 gives an overview of present-day Gothic and explains the reason for the unprecedented popularity this culture currently enjoys.

Part 1: From Ancient Fears to Modern Aesthetics

Chapter 1.1: A Bit of History

The precise definition of the Gothic has always been elusive, and there are as many opinions as experts on this matter. Throughout history, the words "Goth" and "Gothic" were used to describe very different things. Originally, the Goths were one of the tribes that contributed to the fall of the Western Roman Empire. David Punter and Glennis Byron explain:

> The Goths made their first incursion into Roman territory during the third century, and eventually, under Alaric, took Rome in AD 410, subsequently establishing kingdoms in France and Italy. The first extant history of the Goths is Jordanes's *Getica* (551), and here an etymological confusion begins. [. . .] 'Gothic' became a highly mobile term, remaining constant only in the way it functioned to establish a set of polarities revolving primarily around the concepts of the primitive and the civilized. (David Punter and Glennis Byron, *The Gothic.* Blackwell Publishing, 2004, page 3)

During the Renaissance, art historians were using the word "Gothic" as a synonym of "medieval" or "barbaric". This term was initially associated with the idea of a society dominated by superstition and fear; however, its meaning started to change when the perception of medieval history grew more positive. The term "Gothic art" is now used to describe the style that prevailed in Western and Central Europe between the 12th and the 15th centuries. It is no coincidence that Horace Walpole set the story of *The Castle of Otranto* in that period.

Then, what *is* the Gothic culture? This question will not find a straightforward and consensual answer any time soon, and there is no authority able to rule on this matter. Should we apply this term to the Goths who defeated Rome, to all "barbarians" in general, or to the medieval period? In reality, the architectural style called "Gothic" had nothing to do with the ancient Gothic tribes; the builders who perfected this style were calling it "French" or "ogival" (from the Old French "augive" meaning "diagonal rib of a vault" or "pointed arch").

The Gothic culture as we know it today is a modern, post-Renaissance phenomenon, even though its roots stretch back to antiquity. Ironically, Edmund Burke, whose theories provided the philosophical basis for the Gothic fiction, held little esteem for the ancient Goths, as we will see in Chapter 1.3. The origins of the modern Gothic are to be found in the Classical culture. The most influential works were those by Homer, Virgil and Ovid, as well as Greek tragedies. Mythological themes and motifs that appear in Homer's *Iliad* and *Odyssey,* Virgil's *Aeneid,* and Ovid's *Metamorphoses* have never lost their appeal; moreover, these works provided the prototypes of storytelling techniques still used today.

Medieval authors also left their mark on the Gothic culture. Traditionally, their main sources of inspiration were legends, Christian faith and chivalry. Chrétien de Troyes (late 12th century) created the legend of the Grail (in *Perceval, the Story of the Grail*) that inspired countless interpretations and adaptations throughout centuries, a trend that continues unabated today. In the early 14th century, Dante Alighieri wrote one of the most monumental works in history, namely the *Divine Comedy*, describing an imaginary voyage through Hell, Purgatory, and Heaven. In *Inferno,* we already find some elements that will later characterize the Gothic fiction: dark and sublime atmosphere, bestiary of monstrosities from various mythologies, grandiose and dramatic landscapes, stories of love, hate and sin.

The Crusades significantly affected the medieval society; nevertheless, the contact with the Muslim world brought not only war, but also the rediscovery of ancient philosophical and esoteric texts. This triggered a slow but profound change in the medieval culture. Universities were established, new theories emerged, and philosophy was no longer considered incompatible with faith. Aristotle became the new superstar among the cultural elite. Europe was ready for the Renaissance.

The Black Death that struck Europe in the 1340s stopped this cultural process in its tracks. In some countries, up to two-thirds of the population were killed. This traumatic event may explain the fascination with death we find in late medieval art. In the 15th century, the allegorical artistic genre called "Dance of Death" was popular.

Hartmann Schedel, *Nuremberg Chronicle*, 1493

And what about medieval music? Let's mention the troubadours, those famous bards of courtly love, those libertines whose lyrical flights often earned the wrath of clergy and nobles. We should also mention poems that could be sung, for example *Carmina Burana,* or *Songs of Beuren*. Some of them were set to music in the 20th century, first by Carl Orff in 1936, then by several other composers and musical groups.

One might think the spirit of the Renaissance, being subjugated by the love of Classical art, was hardly compatible with medieval culture. In reality, some of the most famous writers from the Renaissance period drew inspiration from the Middle Ages. In *Don Quixote* (1605) Miguel de Cervantes brilliantly shows the ambiguous relationship Europe had with its past. On the one hand, the fascination with the values of chivalry was still alive; however, what fueled this fascination was not a genuine interest in medieval history, but a longing for a glorious, imaginary past. Alonso Quixano, alias Don Quixote, is not trying to revive chivalry; he is trying to live a fantasy inspired by the idealism of old ballads and romances.

The 17th century was the golden age of theater. Guillén de Castro's play *Las mocedades del Cid* (1618) is interesting for two reasons. First, because it shows the influence of medieval ballads on theatrical drama; El Cid was the 11th-century champion of the *Reconquista* (reconquest of Spain by the Christians) celebrated in traditional songs and poems. Second, because it inspired Pierre Corneille's famous tragedy *Le Cid* (1637). Despite its resounding success, *Le Cid* was criticized by the Prime Minister of France, Cardinal de Richelieu, as not observing the "classical unities" and by the French Academy as "dramatically implausible and morally defective".

While in some countries like France artistic creation was hindered by the straitjacket of Classicism, in England theatrical drama was characterized by its boldness and grittiness. Crimes, revenge, murders, suicides, madness – the English audience was spared nothing. The supernatural was also invited to the party, contributing to this dark atmosphere for which Shakespeare's plays – in particular *Hamlet* and *Macbeth* – are so famous. This taste for the macabre owed little to Classicism; it was the heritage of the late medieval culture. Yet, English plays were not sensationalist or medievalist. What Christopher Marlowe, William Shakespeare, John Webster and others created on stage was the forerunner of Gothic fiction, a blend of "the ancient and the modern", a formula Walpole would be using a century and a half later.

At first glance, Shakespeare's *A Midsummer Night's Dream* and Edmund Spenser's *The Faerie Queene* could be classified as fantasy. Both were written in the last decade of the 16th century, both were inspired by legends and folklore, both were animated by a vivid imagination, both were suffused with the supernatural. Both will have a decisive influence on Gothic fantasy and Romanticism, but for different reasons. In *A Midsummer Night's Dream*, everything is in the title: it is a dream. The audience is not prompted to meditate on the "meaning" of this play; there is no hidden message, just a delightful dreamy aesthetic we are invited to enjoy. *The Faerie Queene,* on the other hand, was written with a particular goal: to legitimize the reign of the Protestant Queen Elizabeth I, presented as the monarch of all virtues. Ironically, two centuries later, this poem will be valued as a work connecting modernity with the medieval past the Protestant Reformation tried to destroy.

Castles, ghosts, witches, manipulative aristocrats, secrets, plots, revenge, dreams, stories of impossible love – all the ingredients of Gothic novels were already present in the 16th- and 17th-century plays and poems. Marlowe's *Doctor Faustus* featured a demon, Mephistopheles, and, in *Paradise Lost* (1667), John Milton went even further and gave voice to Satan himself. Now that the last pillar of this infernal temple was in place, everything was ready for the coming of the modern Gothic. All that was needed was a shift in aesthetic tastes, and this shift occurred in the middle of the 18th century.

Chapter 1.2: Gothic Revival

The intellectuals of the Age of Enlightenment did not like the past, the Classical period being an exception to this rule. Everything else – especially the medieval period – was considered a barbaric era, the scars of which were to be erased. Medieval fantasies were discarded as fruits of superstition, the remnants of times gone by. The word "Gothic" was pejorative and used as a synonym of "obscurantist" or "uncivilized".

In England, attempts to break with the past had been made in the 16th century by the Reformation. Protestant kings Henry VIII and Edward VI took apart the very foundations of Catholicism in their country, and this dismantlement of social structures was followed by an equally brutal destruction of buildings associated with the "old faith". Nevertheless, this ravaged, vandalized Gothic past continued to haunt England. Ruins of abbeys and churches stood as embarrassing witnesses of this medieval history that, despite its efforts, modernity was powerless to erase.

Louis Daguerre, *The Ruins of Holyrood Chapel*, 1824

By what mysterious stroke of luck did a story filled with ghosts and goblins written by Walpole find favor in the eyes of these rational and enlightened people who were the English of the 18th century? In fact, this success had little to do with luck. The author of *The Castle of Otranto* gave the answer to this question in his letter to Elie de Beaumont:

> After I have talked of the passions, and the natural effusions of the heart, how will you be surprised to find a narrative of the most improbable and absurd adventures! How will you be amazed to hear that a country of whose good sense you have an opinion should have applauded so wild a tale! But you must remember, Sir, that whatever good sense we have, we are not yet in any light chained down to precepts and inviolable laws. All that Aristotle, or his superior

commentators, your authors, have taught us, has not yet sub-dued us to regularity: we still prefer the extravagant beauties of Shakespeare and Milton to the sober and correct march of Pope.

Historians have shown that toward the end of the 18th century European society experienced a reversal of artistic tastes, and this reversal was as dramatic as it was lasting. Three factors that prepared this revolution should be mentioned.

1 – Reflection on the past and the transitory nature of human life.
2 – Revival of Gothic architecture and interest in all things medieval, including tales and ballads.
3 – Opposition to the Classical aesthetic standards and the emergence of Burkian aesthetics (discussed in Chapter 1.3).

Great Britain was at the forefront of this cultural revolution. Paradoxically, the very forces that destroyed so many medieval buildings in the 16th century started to prepare what is now known as the "Gothic revival" as early as the 17th century. What was driving this movement, a sense of guilt or political necessities? At any rate, this desire to renew with the past and find the roots of British national identity, to better assert it, was profound and, at least for some, genuine.

After the political Gothic came the poetic Gothic. The Graveyard Poets (or Churchyard Poets) drew inspiration from all things that usually evoke melancholy, including ruins, old churches, graves, and cemeteries. "The task be mine," wrote Robert Blair in his poem *The Grave* (1743), "to paint the gloomy horrors of the tomb." Other well-known works belonging to this school are *The Seasons* (1726) by James Thomson, *Night Thoughts* (1742) by Edward Young, and, most famously, *Elegy Written in a Country Churchyard* (1751) by Thomas Gray. Although those poems were meditative and philosophical, they developed an imagery later used in Gothic novels, including references to the supernatural.

The Gothic revival in architecture gained momentum toward the middle of the 18th century. At first, this revival had ideological motives. At that moment in history, the Gothic style was perceived by some as a symbol of British national identity (which is ironic given the fact that this style came initially from France). Being a "Goth" was not only a matter of taste; it was also political statement. In his letter to H S Conway (Chief Secretary for Ireland), Walpole declared: "However rebel this may sound at your court, my Gothic spirit is hurt; I do not love such loyal expressions from a Parliament. I do not so much consider myself writing to Dublin castle, as from Strawberry castle, where you know how I love to enjoy my liberty." In this letter, the choice of words is significant: the "Gothic spirit" is associated with the idea of rebellion against tyrannical authority.

Nevertheless, the tone Walpole uses in his letters to describe Gothic buildings suggests that his admiration for this architectural style was mostly due to his aesthetic tastes rather than politics. In 1750, he wrote: "Soon after my arrival in town I visited Westminster Abbey: the moment I entered I felt a kind of awe pervade my mind which I cannot describe; the very silence seemed sacred. Henry VII's chapel is a very fine piece of Gothic architecture." His works, starting with *Anecdotes of Painting in England* (1762), confirm his emotional attachment to this style.

In the *Letters on Chivalry and Romance* (1762), Richard Hurd also defended medieval architecture: "When an architect examines a Gothic structure by Grecian rules, he finds nothing but deformity. But the Gothic architecture has its own rules, by which, when it comes to be examined, it is seen to have its merit, as well as the Grecian. The question is not which of the two is constructed in the simplest or truest taste: but, whether there be not sense and design in both, when scrutinized by the laws on which each is projected." This British enthusiasm for medieval art spread across Europe. Johann Wolfgang von Goethe voiced a similar opinion in his essay *On German Architecture* (1772), and, later, François-René de Chateaubriand also celebrated the Gothic art in *The Genius of Christianity* (1802).

This passion for old buildings leads to a more general interest in medieval culture and folklore. In the second half of the 18th century, tales and ballads were rediscovered, published and read by a growing audience of enthusiasts. The *Reliques of Ancient English Poetry* (1765), a collection compiled by Thomas Percy, became popular and joined the classics of medieval literature such as *Canterbury Tales* (14th century) by Geoffrey Chaucer and *Le Morte d'Arthur* (1470) by Thomas Malory.

It should be noted, however, that medievalism does not equal Gothicism. Gothic authors were not trying to recount medieval tales or fictionalize historical events. This is how Walpole described the genesis of *The Castle of Otranto*: "I waked one morning, in the beginning of last June, from a dream, of which, all I could recover was, that I had thought myself in an ancient castle (a very natural dream for a head filled like mine with Gothic story), and that on the uppermost banister of a great staircase I saw a gigantic hand in armour. In the evening I sat down, and began to write, without knowing in the least what I intended to say or relate."

No mention of history or politics here; the first Gothic novel was inspired by a *dream*. It was a fruit of the subconscious part of the mind. Note the vocabulary Walpole uses to describe his dream: "ancient castle", "great staircase", "gigantic hand". This is not a naturalistic description of his villa at Strawberry Hill, which was relatively small and not "ancient". In his dream, the space-time continuum seems distorted. This is what Gothicism actually is: an artistic technique that distorts the perception of reality to reveal the hidden truth that lies in the unconscious.

Chapter 1.3: Sublime Terrors, or the Aesthetics of the Dark

In his influential work *Cours d'architecture* (1675), the French architect François Blondel stated that "All the pleasure we derive from artistic beauty depends on the observation of rule and measure: on proportion." This classicist view of aesthetics remained dominant in Europe for the most part of the 18th century. Nevertheless, even in the heart of the Age of Enlightenment, so attached to the values of Classicism, some philosophers started to question the legitimacy of those values. In his essay *A Philosophical Enquiry into the Origin of Our Ideas of the Sublime and Beautiful* (1757), Edmund Burke wrote: "I have great reason to doubt, whether beauty be at all an idea belonging to proportion."

For Burke, the beauty is not in the proportions, utility or completeness. In his view, "we must conclude that beauty is, for the greater part, some quality in bodies acting mechanically upon the human mind by the intervention of the senses." In other words, an object is beautiful only by its action on our mind, not by its intrinsic qualities. It is the *emotion* it produces in us that makes it beautiful.

Another key claim Burke is making relates to the distinction between the beautiful and the sublime. Beauty evokes "positive" emotions such as joy, while the sublime can evoke emotions usually considered "negative" such as sadness or fear. Moreover, for Burke, suffering can also be considered a positive emotion. "For my part, I am rather inclined to imagine, that pain and pleasure, in their most simple and natural manner of affecting, are each of a positive nature, and by no means necessarily dependent on each other for their existence." The author explains that suffering can be "positive" because it is not opposed to pleasure, but to indifference. He goes even further and states that suffering can be a source of pleasure.

No, we're not talking about masochism, but about the noblest form of artistic expression: tragedy. If the stories told by Homer and Greek tragedies are so moving, it is because they conjure up deep and intense emotions such as sorrow and grief. Of all the strong emotions, Burke stresses the importance of fear: "Whatever is fitted in any sort to excite the ideas of pain and danger, that is to say, whatever is in any sort terrible, or is conversant about terrible objects, or operates in a manner analogous to terror, is a source of the sublime; that is, it is productive of the strongest emotion which the mind is capable of feeling."

According to Burke, objects of terror can be of aesthetic value, and this is what makes his essay revolutionary. He develops a set of artistic values centered not around the search for beauty and virtue, but around strong emotions.

At this point, it may be useful to clarify what Burke meant by "terror". In the 18th century, this word did not have the political meaning it has today, although anything considered "alien" or "barbaric" (Gothic!) could be a source of terror. Burke does not mention the Goths in his essay on aesthetics, but he does so in his other writings, so we know his opinion on this matter.

> But there have been periods when no less than universal destruction to the race of mankind seems to have been threatened. Such was that when the Goths, the Vandals, and

the Huns, poured into Gaul, Italy, Spain, Greece, and Africa, carrying destruction before them as they advanced, and leaving horrid deserts every way behind them. (*The Works of the Right Honourable Edmund Burke,* Vol. I)

Nowadays, we know that this was not true, but Burke was the son of his time and shared the common view that "barbarians" could only bring destruction (in reality, the Goths brought probably less destruction than the Roman Empire itself).

Burke's definition of "terror" is broad and encompasses anything from the basic instinct of self-preservation to subtler feelings such as the fear of solitude, the fear of radical social change or the fear of the unknown. One of the most important elements of terror is darkness, as he explains in Part II, Section III:

To make anything very terrible, obscurity seems in general to be necessary. When we know the full extent of any danger, when we can accustom our eyes to it, a great deal of the apprehension vanishes. Every one will be sensible of this, who considers how greatly night adds to our dread, in all cases of danger, and how much the notions of ghosts and goblins, of which none can form clear ideas, affect minds which give credit to the popular tales concerning such sorts of beings.

Because of the importance Burke gives to darkness as the source of sublime, we can call the theory he developed the "aesthetics of the dark". However, in Burke's view, the notion of "terror" encompasses many elements, including mystery, danger, privations ("ALL *general* privations are great, because they are all terrible; *vacuity, darkness, solitude,* and *silence*"), vastness, infinity, difficulty, magnificence, color (his preference goes to black, brown and deep purple), loudness and suddenness of sounds, as well as all kinds of unpleasant feelings, including pain. These are just some of the examples mentioned in Burke's essay. Besides its philosophical ambitions, this work can be useful to any writer, artist or filmmaker as it gives suggestions and examples of how to create a dark and frightening atmosphere in a work of fiction.

Chapter 1.4: The Gothic as a Literary Style

The Gothic novel became the first application of Burkian theories; the first in a long series of popular successes. This genre exploded in England and other European countries in the 1790s. The term "Gothic novel" was coined retrospectively by 20th-century critics and was applied to the works that followed more or less the same formula. Their plot was set in a distant past (medieval period or Renaissance) and involved some dreadful secret or romantic intrigue (often both). The list of main characters included a villain (aristocrat or cleric), a young and vulnerable heroine, and a valiant "Prince Charming" she unavoidably fell in love with. All sorts of frightening experiences awaited the protagonists, and Gothic buildings (castles, churches, abbeys) always contained secret passages and skeletons hidden in chests and closets.

Despite its initial success, this genre had a relatively short life span. The number of new "frightening" books declined in the 1810s and, in the 1820s, the Gothic novel was already out of fashion. While stories about haunted castles were starting to lose their appeal, a new breed of "terrifying" tales made its appearance and dark Romanticism was born. The first authors to venture into this uncharted territory were E T A Hoffmann in Germany and Lord Byron in Great Britain. The latter was joined in this journey by his friends John William Polidori, Mary Shelley and Percy Bysshe Shelley.

Dark Romanticism was instrumental in shaping the modern Gothic culture. Technically, dark Romantic works do not belong to the Gothic genre; nevertheless, their aesthetic is unmistakably Gothic. This distinction between a *genre* and an *artistic style* is subtle, but all-important in this context. A genre is defined by its motifs and conventions; a style is defined by a set of aesthetic values. There are no haunted castles or manipulative villains in Mary Shelley's *Frankenstein*, and the story is not set in a distant past, therefore it cannot be categorized as a Gothic novel. On the other hand, this work was written according to the aesthetic principles defined by Burke, Walpole and Radcliffe, therefore it has its place in the Gothic culture.

Characteristics of the Literary Gothic

The Gothic aesthetic often works by establishing an arresting contrast between the beautiful and the sublime. The canonical image associated with the 18th-century Gothic novel is that of a young and vulnerable heroine escaping a dark and sinister castle. The woman is invariably beautiful; the castle is invariably "sublime", which means "terrifying".

> The lower part of the castle was hollowed into several intricate cloisters; and it was not easy for one under so much anxiety to find the door that opened into the cavern. An awful silence reigned throughout those subterraneous regions, except now and then some blasts of wind that shook the doors she had passed, and which, grating on the rusty hinges, were re-echoed through that long labyrinth of darkness. Every murmur struck her with new terror; yet more she dreaded to hear the wrathful voice of Manfred urging his domestics to pursue her.
>
> She trod as softly as impatience would give her leave, yet frequently stopped and listened to hear if she was followed. In one of those moments she thought she heard a sigh. She shuddered, and recoiled a few paces. In a moment she thought she heard the step of some person. Her blood curdled; she concluded it was Manfred. Every suggestion that horror could inspire rushed into her mind. (Horace Walpole, *The Castle of Otranto*, 1764)

Note the vocabulary of fear Walpole uses: "anxiety", "awful", "darkness", "terror", "dreaded", "wrathful", "she shuddered, and recoiled", "horror". As an artistic style, the Gothic is particularly suitable to create suspense. This technique is widely used nowadays, in particular in films, where the anticipation of danger is as frightening as the object of terror itself. It is also often used in present-day literature, especially in thrillers, horror fiction and urban fantasy.

The Gothic artistic style is also used to create an atmosphere where the sense of danger is somehow subdued; there is no immediate threat, but we know it is there, lurking in the shadows. Edgar Allan Poe is famous for his mastery of this technique.

During the whole of a dull, dark, and soundless day in the autumn of the year, when the clouds hung oppressively low in the heavens, I had been passing alone, on horseback, through a singularly dreary tract of country, and at length found myself, as the shades of the evening drew on, within view of the melancholy House of Usher. I know not how it was – but, with the first glimpse of the building, a sense of insufferable gloom pervaded my spirit. I say insufferable; for the feeling was unrelieved by any of that half-pleasurable, because poetic, sentiment, with which the mind usually receives even the sternest natural images of the desolate or terrible. (Edgar Allan Poe, *The Fall of the House of Usher*, 1839)

Again, note the vocabulary: "dull", "dark", "autumn", "oppressively", "alone", "dreary", "shades", "melancholy", "insufferable gloom", "desolate", "terrible". Poe's works are outstanding applications of Burkian theories, and it is not surprising that they continue to inspire countless authors, artists and musicians.

For Burke, the notion of "horror" covers much more than just fear. He explains: "The passion caused by the great and sublime in *nature*, when those causes operate most powerfully, is astonishment: and astonishment is that state of the soul in which all its motions are suspended, with some degree of horror."

This observation brings us to the next point, the importance of the landscape in Gothic fiction. The tradition of associating the physical landscape with the mental one was not new in the 18th century. Celtic and medieval legends are interesting in this regard. Heroes are astonished by an impressive sight – a dark enchanted forest, a castle erected at the top of a mountain, a tower leaning above the abyss – even before they meet the inhabitants of this forest, castle or tower. The décor is already preparing us for the events to come by creating the appropriate atmosphere. The masters of Gothic fiction, horror and fantasy understood the importance of the landscape. For example, Ann Radcliffe's descriptions are particularly vivid:

The solitary grandeur of the objects that immediately surrounded her, the mountain-region towering above, the deep

precipices that fell beneath, the waving blackness of the forests of pine and oak, which skirted their feet, or hung within
their recesses, the headlong torrents that, dashing among
their cliffs, sometimes appeared like a cloud of mist, at others
like a sheet of ice — these were features which received a
higher character of sublimity from the reposing beauty of the
Italian landscape below, stretching to the wide horizon,
where the same melting blue tint seemed to unite earth and
sky.

Madame Montoni only shuddered as she looked down precipices near whose edge the chairmen trotted lightly and
swiftly, almost, as the chamois bounded, and from which
Emily too recoiled; but with her fears were mingled such various emotions of delight, such admiration, astonishment, and
awe, as she had never experienced before. (Ann Radcliffe, *The
Mysteries of Udolpho*, 1794)

In this passage, the same vocabulary is used not to describe dread,
but awe. Our heroines "shudder" and "recoil" with "fear"; however,
this time, the source of fear is not danger but "sublimity" that causes
"delight", "admiration, astonishment, and awe". In Gothic fiction, the
notions of "terror" and "horror" encompass all those emotions.

Chapter 1.5: The Gothic in Visual Arts

The Gothic extensively uses visual codes, some of which remained constant throughout its history, while others evolved, but remain
recognizable today. The first of those visual codes came from architecture. The Gothic revival occurred in several stages. In the middle of the
18th century, old castles were restored and new ones were built mainly
by the prominent members of the Whig party, often to serve as a political statement (see Chapter 1.2). Strawberry Hill was a relatively small
project attempting to Gothicize a villa initially built in a classical style.
The time of ambitious projects came in the 19th century; two of the most
typical examples of neo-Gothic architecture in London are the Palace of
Westminster, rebuilt after being devastated by the fire of 1834, and St

Pancras train station.

John Rutter, *Delineations of Fonthill and its Abbey,* 1823, Plate 11

To the south-west of London, Fonthill Abbey was commissioned in 1796 by William Thomas Beckford, the author of the Orientalist Gothic novel *Vathek* (1786). The building collapsed in 1825, but drawings of it survived thanks to John Rutter's *Delineations of Fonthill and its Abbey* (1823). Plate 11 shows this castle in all its dark beauty, its three hundred foot tall tower stretching to the sky. One can feel an almost supernatural energy projected by this tower; people are dwarfed by it, clouds are swirling around it like evil spirits. This drawing illustrates Burkian statements about the sublimity of vastness (Edmund Burke, *A Philosophical Enquiry . . . ,* Part II, Section VII).

While Walpole was drawing the plans of his Gothic villa, in Italy, Giovanni Battista Piranesi was working on a series of sixteen prints called *The Prisons*. These visionary etchings were inspired by Gothic architecture and depicted dark, claustrophobic, sometimes surreal places.

A century later, the works by Gustave Doré, French engraver and illustrator, cultivated a similar atmosphere. The latter illustrated the Bible, Dante's *Divine Comedy*, Milton's *Paradise Lost*, fairy tales, and the books by some of the greatest Romantic authors: Byron, Coleridge, Chateaubriand, Théophile Gautier, Edgar Allan Poe. The hallmark of Doré's art is his masterful use of contrast; he was able to shape light and darkness to create a feeling of scale and grandeur.

In painting, the most influential artists inspired by the Gothic were Henry Fuseli, Francisco Goya, William Blake and Caspar David Friedrich. Fuseli's painting *The Nightmare* (1781) became associated with the Gothic culture and still inspires artists. The same motif appears in Goya's famous work *The Sleep of Reason Produces Monsters* (1799). The epigraph for this etching reads: "Imagination abandoned by reason produces impossible monsters; united with her, she is the mother of the arts and source of their wonders." Goya's interest in the supernatural inspired several paintings such as *Witches' Sabbath* (1798), *Witches' Flight* (1798), and the second *Witches' Sabbath* or *The Great He-Goat* (1821-23). The latter was part of a group of fourteen works collectively known as *The Black Paintings*, the most well-known of them being *Saturn Devouring His Son* (1819-23).

Blake was also passionate about the supernatural, but for a different reason. While Fuseli's and Goya's art can be viewed as an exploration of psychological states, Blake's works are essentially mystical. Colors, fantastical shapes, monsters, angels and demons – his works are filled with energy, movement, and passion. Blake's art could be qualified as "fantastical expressionism", a forerunner of the Expressionist Movement (we will come back to Expressionism in a moment).

Caspar David Friedrich, *Monastery Graveyard in the Snow*, 1819

Caspar David Friedrich, a renowned German painter from the Romantic period, took a different approach to spirituality. He depicted churches, graves, ruins, old trees, crosses and anything sublime in a Burkian sense. He gave the Gothic its canonical imagery in paintings such as *The Abbey in the Oakwood* (1809-10) and *Monastery Graveyard in the Snow* (1819). The hallmark of Friedrich's works is a particular atmosphere filled with mystery and melancholy. The landscape is not just a background, it is *the object*; it represents the inner, mental, emotional landscape of the artist, which is again consistent with the Burkian definition of beauty. Romanticism heralded artistic movements such as Symbolism, Surrealism and Expressionism, where the lines between "the real" and "the felt" fade away. The French Symbolist Paul Verlaine starts his poem *Clair de Lune* (1869) with the following statement: "Your soul is a chosen landscape", then he goes on to describe what we might call a fantasy scenery.

As mentioned in the previous chapter, this idea of an intimate connection between the landscape and the "soul", the mental landscape, has its origins in Gothic fiction. The haunted castle with all its horrors can be viewed as a projection of the corrupt and malevolent psyche of its master. The castle becomes a character in its own right. The skeletons hidden in chests and closets symbolize repressed desires, ghosts represent unconscious fears, and monsters are manifestations of the uncanny in the Freudian sense.

In his essay *Das Unheimliche*, Sigmund Freud defines the uncanny as "that class of the frightening which leads back to what is known of old and long familiar". Gothic monsters are not frightening because they are alien – they are frightening because our unconscious mind recognizes them. This concept is key to understanding how the Gothic aesthetics influenced 20th-century culture.

Illustration: Gothic nightmares; Henry Fuseli, *The Nightmare*, 1781 (top); Francisco de Goya, *The Sleep of Reason Produces Monsters*, 1799 (bottom left); William Blake, *The Great Red Dragon and the Woman Clothed in Sun*, 1806-1809 (bottom right).

Gothic on Screen

Cinema fell in love with the Gothic from the beginning, and this romance has grown stronger over the decades. Since *The Haunted Castle* (*Le Manoir du Diable*, Georges Méliès, 1896), Gothic motifs and imagery have haunted the screen. Mary Shelley's *Frankenstein* alone has inspired about thirty movies, the first one being the version directed by J Searle Dawley in 1910. In the 1920s and 30s, the German Expressionist film drew heavily on the Gothic. Expressionism is usually defined as an art of self-expression where artists depict not the objective reality, but their emotional response to this reality.

The most influential Expressionist films were *The Cabinet of Dr Caligari* (Robert Wiene, 1920), *Nosferatu, a Symphony of Horror* (F W Murnau, 1922, the first adaptation of Stoker's *Dracula*), and *Metropolis* (Fritz Lang, 1927). Among other movies influenced by the Gothic, we could mention *Genuine* (Wiene, 1920), *The Golem* (Paul Wegener, 1920), *Weary Death* (Lang, 1921), *Dr Mabuse, the Gambler* (Lang, 1922), *The Doll Maker of Kiang-Ning* (Wiene, 1923), and *The Nibelungen: Siegfried* and *Kriemhild's Revenge* (Lang, 1924).

Metropolis, a bleak, yet sublime vision of technological society, is among the most impressive movies of the silent era. The Gothic influenced this film at several levels. Some of these influences are obvious, like the scenes where Rotwang, a mad scientist, chases Maria in the catacombs or in the cathedral; some of them revolve around the imagery related to religion, sin, fear, and death. Some of them are subtler.

The masterful use of contrast between light and darkness is a hallmark of Expressionist film. This technique, called *chiaroscuro*, was initially developed by the Renaissance artists and was also extensively used by Piranesi, Goya, and Doré. In one scene from *Metropolis* we see Freder, son of the leader of the city, standing in the background, bathed in light, when a dark procession carrying injured and dead workers marches before the camera. In general, the aesthetic of this film works precisely in accordance with Gothic tradition, by creating a contrast between the sublime (the frightening and the uncanny) and the beautiful. For example, the contrast between the lower and upper cities could not be more striking. The former is dark, gloomy, claustrophobic; it has no place for creativity. The latter is filled with light, optimism and fanciful beauty. To Freder, the lower city appears hellish, demonic. The suffering of its workers is physical, palpable. The uncanny machine is assimilated with Moloch, an ancient god who required human sacrifice. Like Saturn in Goya's painting, Metropolis devours its children.

Christian and satanic symbolism are found throughout this film. Maria is presented as a saint, and she preaches surrounded by Christian crosses and icons. In contrast, the first time we see the "female" robot created by Rotwang, she has for background an inverted pentagram. Later, people will call her a witch and burn her at the stake. Nevertheless, *Metropolis* is not a film about religion, and its message is rather psychological: "The mediator between head and hands must be the heart!"

To conclude this brief analysis, we might say that the Gothic visual codes underpin the psychological, even psychoanalytical aspect of this film; they allow subversion of reality to reveal the hidden, unconscious truth. *Metropolis* is essentially a satire, drawing a grotesque, yet recognizable picture of German society in the 1920s. A childishly naïve Freder and a theatrically heroic Maria are opposed to larger-than-life characters such as a comically devilish Rotwang and his wicked robot. Fritz Lang offers us some delightful moments of dark humor, when, for example, the statue symbolizing Death starts to dance and plays flute using a bone as a musical instrument. Other scenes are overwhelmingly powerful, in particular toward the end of the film, when the upper class engages in extravagant celebrations, oblivious to the social upheaval that reigns in the depths of the city. Such was the Weimar Republic, naïve, torn between the contemplation of its Gothic past and its fascination with technology and industrialism. Released two years before the Great Depression and five years before Hitler came to power, *Metropolis* was not only visionary – it was prophetic.

Silent films were instrumental in defining Gothic visual codes we now find in every visual art form and media: cinema, TV, graphic novel, digital art, and even computer games (further discussed in Part 3). TV series such as *The Twilight Zone, Dark Shadows, Tales from the Crypt* or *X-Files* offer some interesting examples. Moreover, the Gothic suffused popular culture to such an extent that we find it in most unexpected places.

To take just one example, let's mention the TV series *Smallville* (2001-11). *A priori,* this series has nothing to do with the Gothic tradition; it tells the story of how Clark Kent became Superman. Nevertheless, *Smallville* often uses Gothic motifs and imagery. The past coming back to haunt the present is one of the main motifs. "You are just a voice, Jor-El, an echo from the past", utters a phantom who took Clark's appearance in *Persona* (Season 7, Episode 10). Events that took place years ago on his home planet continue to irrupt into Clark's life, threatening not only him, but entire humanity. In *Apocalypse* (Season 7, Episode 18), Jor-El transports Clark to an alternative universe to show him what life would have been if he had not existed, and the story ends with a global atomic conflict. The message is clear: Kryptonians destroyed their planet, and now Earth is in danger. "Crypto" comes from Greek *kruptos,* which means secret, hidden. Krypton symbolizes our collective unconscious, in particular our fear of self-destruction. The Cold War may be over, but its ghost still haunts us.

The influence of the Gothic on cinema and TV is further discussed in Chapter 3.1.

Chapter 1.6: The Gothic in Modern Music

In the 20th century, two inventions revolutionized popular music: the electric guitar and the synthesizer. The first electric guitars were commercialized in the early 1930s and were mainly used by jazz musicians. In the 1950s, improved versions of this instrument allowed the emergence of rock and roll; without this invention, popular music as we know it would not exist. In the 1970s, the synthesizer opened the door on a new universe of creativity and unleashed a wave of musical experimentation.

Rock bands embraced the synthesizer from the early 1970s, the album *Who's Next* (1971) by The Who being one of the most famous examples, in particular the opening track *Baba O'Riley*. The experimentation conducted by Pink Floyd was more sophisticated. The track *On the Run* from the album *The Dark Side of the Moon* (1973) was stunning, given the limited technology available then. Vangelis, whose name will later be associated with epic electronic music, started his career in the late 1960s by founding the progressive rock band Aphrodite's Child. However, his interest gradually shifted from rock to more classically-inspired music. *Heaven and Hell* (1975) was a milestone in this journey, as it still bore the imprint of psychedelic rock, but already contained the elements that later brought Vangelis a worldwide fame, notably his masterful use of the synthesizer. The first album by the French composer Jean Michel Jarre, *Deserted Palace* (1972), was far from being successful, but his third album, *Oxygen* (1976), was a marvel of an otherworldly beauty and became a classic of electronic music.

The 70s also witnessed the explosion of an edgy, rebellious and politicized genre of rock. "Explosion" is the right word, as the punk movement rose to celebrity as quickly as it lost its momentum. In England, several bands that were originally part of this movement tried to develop new, alternative aesthetics. They combined the energy of the punk with the atmospheric sound of the synthesizer to create a more elaborate, experimental, and often dissonant music.

Siouxsie and the Banshees can be credited for launching the post-punk movement with their song "Hong Kong Garden" and their first album *The Scream* (1978). The fact that the lead singer of this band was a woman is significant, and we will come back to this point in Chapter 2.5. Another key figure in the history of post-punk is Ian Curtis of Joy Division. More than a singer, he was also a composer and a poet in the noblest sense of this term. Passionate about literature, he read Gogol, Dostoevsky, Nietzsche, Hermann Hesse, Kafka, H P Lovecraft, Jean-Paul Sartre. He enjoyed SF, in particular William S Burroughs and J G Ballard. Reading was not only a hobby to him; it was part of his work, and we find several literary references in his songs.

Joy Division released two studio albums, *Unknown Pleasures* (1979) and *Closer* (1980), before its existence ended in tragedy. In 1980, when he was only 23, Ian Curtis committed suicide. *Closer* was his masterpiece, edgy and atmospheric, filled with dark poetry. The lyrics of songs such as "Heart and Soul" remind us of Lovecraft and his bleak view of our future.

In the 1980s, post-punk branched into countless streams and each of them was a musical genre in its own right. Bands such as The Cure and Depeche Mode had their "dark" periods at the beginning of the 1980s before turning to more optimistic musical styles. These bands never considered themselves "Gothic", although one may argue that the albums *Seventeen Seconds* (1980), *Faith* (1981) and *Pornography* (1982) by The Cure, and *Black Celebration* (1986) by Depeche Mode belong to the Goth subculture. A similar comment can be made about The Sisters of Mercy.

Goth rock originated mainly from post-punk, although the influences of glam rock and new romanticism should also be noted. The band often credited with the creation of Goth rock, Bauhaus, drew on distinctly Gothic sources. Their first song, "Bela Lugosi's Dead" (1979), was a homage to the actor famous for portraying Dracula in the eponymous film directed by Tod Browning (1931). The Batcave, an underground night-club located in Soho in Central London became the hub of the budding Goth subculture. This club opened in 1982 and bands such as Bauhaus, Alien Sex Fiend, Specimen, Foetus and others performed there. Historically, Soho is associated with Charles Dickens and his novels, and it was also the hub of bohemian life in postwar London, so its location was symbolic and contributed to the creation of the right atmosphere.

The greatest achievement of the Goth movement was to create a sense of unity, a sense of belonging to a culture rooted in artistic tradition. For the first time in history, the term "Gothic" was not applied to a movement retrospectively. Paradoxically, when Bauhaus was composing *Bela Lugosi's Dead*, the Gothic culture had been around for two centuries, yet its existence had never been acknowledged outside a small circle of connoisseurs and critics.

How can we define Gothic music? In a broad sense, any music that has a dark and mysterious feel to it might be qualified as Gothic. Nothing prevents us from applying this term to classically-inspired music such as the original scores for German Expressionist films. Gottfried Huppertz, for example, who collaborated with Fritz Lang, wrote sublime sound tracks with distinctive Gothic undertones. In the same manner, we can apply this term to some albums by Vangelis (*Heaven and Hell*, score for the film *Blade Runner*) and other modern composers.

A narrow definition would include only rock bands that openly claim to belong to the Goth movement. This would apply to Clan of Xymox, Fields of the Nephilim, Inkubus Sukkubus, London After Midnight, and The Crüxshadows, to name just a few. This would also include Christian Death, Faith and the Muse, and other death rock bands. However, it would be a shame to content ourselves with such a restrictive definition and ignore all the musical diversity that flourished under the influence of the Gothic culture.

The prevalent features of this kind of music are:

- An atmosphere that cultivates the aesthetic of the dark.
- A contrast between the beautiful and the sublime.
- An interest in the traditional Gothic themes such as the supernatural and the afterlife.
- A reflection on the past (for example, Middle Ages, Victorian period, World War Two).

Although the synthesizer had an important role in the history of Gothic music, some bands replaced it with traditional instruments. This return to a more "natural" sound is an interesting trend in present-day rock. Since the 1980s, the synthesizer has been increasingly associated with pop music, and rock bands often want to differentiate themselves from synthpop.

Another interesting trend is the blending of rock with symphonic and traditional music. Dead Can Dance experimented with this approach from 1981, inspiring a new genre called neoclassical Gothic or neoclassical darkwave. Even though Arcana, Dark Sanctuary, Nox Arcana, Autumn Tears, and other "dark" neoclassical bands are not particularly famous, their influence on the evolution of alternative rock and metal was significant. We will discuss this further in Chapter 3.2.

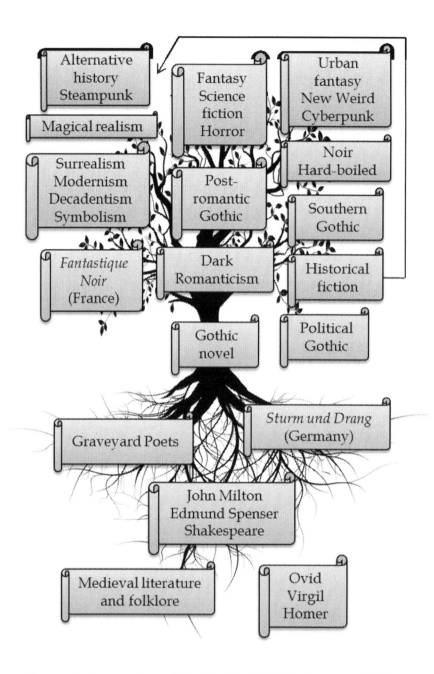

The evolutionary tree of the Gothic. ©A J Blakemont, 2014.

Part 2: Gothic Evolution

Chapter 2.1: Evolutionary Tree of the Gothic

The Gothic mutates, the Gothic diversifies, the Gothic crossbreeds; in other words, the Gothic evolves. Sometimes, its new forms are so strange (alien!) that we struggle to recognize them as being part of an artistic tradition that dates from the 18th century. Yet, at least subconsciously, we do recognize them, as their manifestations are both familiar and frightening: they are *uncanny*.

For the last two centuries, Gothic fiction went through a series of transformations, literature being in the forefront of this artistic innovation. Gothic literature developed in several waves:

1 – Gothic novel (1764-1820): Horace Walpole's *The Castle of Otranto* (1764); Clara Reeve's *The Old English Baron* (1778); William Thomas Beckford's *Vathek* (1786); Ann Radcliffe's *The Romance of the Forest* (1791), *The Mysteries of Udolpho* (1794), and *The Italian* (1797); Matthew Gregory Lewis's *The Monk* (1796); Charles Brockden Brown's *Wieland* (1798); Jane Austen's *Northanger Abbey* (written in 1798-99, published in 1818); Charles Maturin's *Melmoth the Wanderer* (1820).

2 – Dark Romanticism (1810s-1850s): E T A Hoffmann's tales, short stories, and novels (1815-22); Lord Byron's *Darkness* (1916), *Manfred* (1817), and other poems; Mary Shelley's *Frankenstein* (1818); John William Polidori's *The Vampyre* (1819); Charles Nodier's tales and short stories (1820s-30s); Théophile Gautier's *The Dead Woman in Love* (1836) and other short stories; Edgar Allan Poe's poems and short stories (1827-49); Victor Hugo's *The Hunchback of Notre Dame* (1831); Honoré de Balzac's *The Magic Skin* (1831); Emily Brontë's *Wuthering Heights* (1847); Charlotte Brontë's *Jane Eyre* (1847); Nathaniel Hawthorne's *The House of the Seven Gables* (1851) and short stories; Gérard de Nerval's *Aurélia*

(1855); Charles Baudelaire's *The Flowers of Evil* (1857).

3 – Post-romantic Gothic (1850s-1910s): Wilkie Collins's *The Woman in White* (1860) and *The Moonstone* (1868); Sheridan Le Fanu's *Uncle Silas* (1864) and *In a Glass Darkly* (1872); Robert Louis Stevenson's *Strange Case of Dr Jekyll and Mr Hyde* (1886); Oscar Wilde's *The Picture of Dorian Gray* (1891); Jules Verne's *The Carpathian Castle* (1892); Arthur Machen's *The Great God Pan* (1894); H G Wells's *The Island of Doctor Moreau* (1896); Bram Stoker's *Dracula* (1897); Henry James's *The Turn of the Screw* (1898); Gaston Leroux's *The Phantom of the Opera* (1910).

4 – Twentieth-century Gothic horror: H P Lovecraft's *The Call of Cthulhu* (1926) and other short stories; Richard Matheson's *I Am Legend* (1954); Robert Bloch's *Psycho* (1960); Stephen King's *Carrie* (1974), *Salem's Lot* (1975), *The Shining* (1977), and other novels; Anne Rice's *Interview with the Vampire* (1976).

5 – Cyberpunk, steampunk, dark fantasy, urban fantasy, supernatural thriller, New Weird: genres and movements that emerged in the 1980s-90s partly under the influence of Gothic culture.

Several influential works not included in one of the categories presented above should also be mentioned: William Godwin's *Caleb Williams* (1794), Washington Irving's short story *The Legend of Sleepy Hollow* (1820), William Faulkner's *Absalom, Absalom!* (1936) and other novels, and Mervyn Peake's *Gormenghast* trilogy (1946-59).

As we can see from this list of works, which is far from being exhaustive, the Gothic literature is surprisingly diverse. The key to its success lies in its ability to reflect the fears and the longings of a particular generation of readers. The rise of the Gothic novel coincided with the time of revolutions: the American Revolution, the French Revolution, the Industrial Revolution. The Reign of Terror in France (1793) contributed to Gothic's popularity by creating an atmosphere of apprehension in the entire Western world.

Dark Romanticism was the next logical step in the evolution of the literature of terror. Romanticism appeared in response to the same anxieties that set in motion the first wave of Gothic fiction; however, it brought the psychological dimension the Gothic novel was lacking. Characters became more complex, settings became more diverse, and the writing style became more sophisticated. Romanticism glorified passion, even in its darkest and destructive forms. Its roots can be found in the German movement *Sturm und Drang* represented mainly by Johann Wolfgang von Goethe and Friedrich Schiller. *The Sorrows of Young Werther* (1774) and *Faust* (1808) in particular influenced dark Romanticism.

In poetry, two 19th-century authors brought the Gothic to new heights (or lows, meaning depths): Edgar Allan Poe in the United States and Charles Baudelaire in France. Both were visionaries, both were ahead of their time, both were misunderstood by their contemporaries. Poe is usually presented as the master of horror fiction, while Baudelaire is known as the father of Symbolism. This view, however, is too restrictive to account for their legacy. Their most enduring achievement was to prepare the transition between Romanticism and post-romantic movements such as Symbolism, Modernism, the Decadent Movement, Expressionism, and Surrealism.

All those movements emerged in response to Realism, as Romanticism had emerged in response to Classicism. While Realists believed that art should reflect the objective reality, Symbolists, Modernists, Expressionists, and Surrealists emphasized their emotional, subjective perception of this reality. The boundaries between real and imaginary, mental health and insanity, the conscious and the unconscious, the primitive and the civilized, the human and the animal, and even the boundaries between life and death were not only to be explored, but crossed and breached (further discussed in Chapters 2.2, 2.3, and 2.4).

Scientific theories, technological progress and social changes brought new interrogations and anxieties. Catherine Crowe wrote in *The Night-side of Nature* (1848): "Scarcely a month passes, that we do not hear of some new and important discovery in science; it is a domain in which nothing is stable; and every year overthrows some of the hasty and premature theories of the preceding ones." This feeling of instability and uncertainty permeated the post-romantic Gothic. For example, Arthur Machen writes in *The Great God Pan:*

> "The skin, and the flesh, and the muscles, and the bones, and the firm structure of the human body that I had thought to be unchangeable, and permanent as adamant, began to melt and dissolve.

"I know that the body may be separated into its elements by external agencies, but I should have refused to believe what I saw. For here there was some internal force, of which I knew nothing, that caused dissolution and change.

"Here too was all the work by which man had been made repeated before my eyes. I saw the form waver from sex to sex, dividing itself from itself, and then again reunited. Then I saw the body descend to the beasts whence it ascended, and that which was on the heights go down to the depths, even to the abyss of all being. The principle of life, which makes organism, always remained, while the outward form changed."

Social and political changes were also a considerable source of anxiety in Victorian and Edwardian Great Britain. Aristocrats and corrupt clergymen who terrorized virgins in Gothic novels were replaced by new, more frightening villains: serial killers, mad scientists, and all sorts of tyrants. The latter gave voice to the collective fear of totalitarian ideologies that developed at the beginning of the 20th century.

World War One and the Great Depression found their echo in Gothic fiction. The word "horror" now had a new meaning, and the old monsters acquired a different symbolic value. The benevolent "invisible hand" the 18th-century liberals believed in was replaced by the invisible hand of doom, a superior force before which humans were powerless and that could reduce any civilization to cinders. Lovecraftian creatures such as Cthulhu are highly symbolic in this regard (further discussed in Chapter 2.4).

Throughout the 20th century, traditional monsters, those inspired by legends and folklore, were joined by new ones. In 1933, King Kong made his sensational entry in the eponymous film directed by Merian C Cooper and Ernest B Schoedsack. The success of this movie can be explained by its imaginative plot and its special effects, and, more importantly, by the unconscious associations it created. Does King Kong symbolize the hidden economic potential of the developing countries? A potential Western powers were seeking to exploit, sometimes ruthlessly. But no chains can restrain this giant; eventually it breaks free, and confrontation is unavoidable.

Urban Gothic

Since the 1930s, another theme has become more and more often associated with Gothic fiction: the urban environment and its underworld. Fritz Lang can be credited with starting this trend with his films *Metropolis* (1927), *The Big Heat* (1953), and others. The urban Gothic branched into several genres. *The Maltese Falcon* (1929) by Dashiell Hammett launched the hard-boiled detective novel, a genre that inspired the film noir popular in the 1940s and 50s. The history of crime fiction can be traced back to dark Romantic works such as *The Murders in the Rue Morgue* (1841) by Edgar Allan Poe, *The Mysteries of Paris* (1842-43) by Eugène Sue, *The Mysteries of London* (1844-56) by G W M Reynolds, and *The Moonstone* (1868) by Wilkie Collins.

Urban SF was never recognized as a distinct subgenre, although it cropped up here and there, sometimes with great effect: *The Caves of Steel* (1954) by Isaac Asimov, *Make Room! Make Room!* (1966) by Harry Harrison, *Stand on Zanzibar* (1969) by John Brunner, *The World Inside* (1971) by Robert Silverberg, *Crash* by J G Ballard (1973), and, more recently, *The City and the City* (2009) by China Miéville. These are just a few examples; see the *Encyclopedia of Science Fiction* for further information (http://www.sf-encyclopedia.com/entry/cities). Urban SF is not necessarily Gothic (although some works by J G Ballard and Iain Banks *are* considered Gothic; see David Punter and Glennis Byron, *The Gothic*, Blackwell Publishing, 2004, 82-4). Nevertheless, the roots of this subgenre intertwine with the history of Gothic fiction, *Metropolis* being one of the examples of this relationship.

Superhero fiction embraced the urban Gothic and integrated it into its fabric. Bob Kane and Bill Finger created a dark and mysterious hero, Batman, who has been haunting popular culture since 1939. In general, comic books often drew on Gothic motifs and imagery, for example in *Tomb of Dracula* (1973) where the vampire hunter Blade appeared for the first time, in *Hellblazer* series, *Hellboy* series, and many others.

All this impressive array of genres, settings and motifs, from *Metropolis* to vampire slayers, from cynical private detectives to superheroes, from social realities of the Great Depression to extraterrestrial cities, stems from the anxieties created by urbanization. While the crimes of Jack the Ripper inspired countless stories about serial killers, Al Capone inspired countless charismatic, yet ruthless fictional crime lords. The urban Gothic deals with any social problems that plague big cities: poverty and social exclusion (Neil Gaiman's *Neverwhere*, 1996), infectious diseases (a recurrent motif since Richard Matheson's *I Am Legend*, 1954), overpopulation and pollution (*Make Room! Make Room!* by Harry Harrison, 1966, Richard Fleischer's film *Soylent Green*, 1973). Multiculturalism, immigration and ethnic segregation are also common themes, for example in Southern Gothic (William Faulkner's *Absalom, Absalom!* and other novels), and urban fantasy (see Chapter 2.2).

Gothicized Technology

Fears related to new technologies have been shaping the Gothic since Mary Shelley's *Frankenstein*. In *Gothic Science Fiction*, Sara Wasson and Emily Alder explain: "Frankenstein's monster is organically revisited as mutant or genetically engineered organism, reworked as artificial intelligence or mechanical construction." (*Gothic Science Fiction 1980–2010*, Edited by Sara Wasson and Emily Alder, Liverpool Science Fiction Texts and Studies 41). The idea that we can create something that would one day revolt and enslave us, or even destroy us, has been haunting SF since the beginning of this genre. This angst took a particularly disturbing form in films such as *The Terminator* (James Cameron, 1984) and *The Matrix* series (The Wachowski Brothers, 1999-2003). The subgenre called cyberpunk emerged in the 80s, William Gibson being the most well-known writer associated with it. In *The Neuromantic Cyberpunks* (*Science Fiction in the Real World*, 1990, Southern Illinois University Press, 109-21), Norman Spinrad characterizes the novel *Neuromancer* (1984) as "a new, forthrightly high-tech, romanticism".

> If the punks of the 1950s really were anti-intellectual hoods, the nouvelle punks of the 1970s were intellectual anti-intellectuals; not naïve natural nihilistic rebels without a cause but self-consciously nihilistic pessimists capable of raising cynicism to a more or less coherent philosophy and sophisticated enough to know they were doing it.

This is probably the most insightful definition of post-punk one can find in a book of literary criticism, and the fact that we find it in an essay on the evolution of SF is no coincidence. Both from a chronological and aesthetic point of view, "cyberpunk" would be better qualified as "cyber-post-punk" or "cybergoth". Chronologically, the development of this subgenre coincided with the rise of the Goth movement; aesthetically, cyberpunk borrowed a lot from the Goth scene, starting with fashion: black clothing, long coats, dark glasses. Both Goths and cyberpunks are dark romantics who embraced modernity and technology, the former rebelling against the aesthetic standards of the consumerist culture and the latter rebelling against a soulless, mechanized society dominated by artificial intelligence. In both cases they fight for their right to express their individuality and reject conformism.

Humorous Gothic

To conclude this overview, we should remind ourselves that the Gothic can also be funny, as Jane Austen showed in her witty parody *Northanger Abbey*. We could distinguish two types of humorous Gothic. The first type would include works that make a mockery of Gothic clichés, like *Northanger Abbey*, the *Scooby-Doo* franchise (first launched as a cartoon series in 1969), or the movie *Beetlejuice* (Tim Burton, 1988). The second type would include works of social satire and dark humor, for example, *The Addams Family* created by American cartoonist Charles Addams, or TV series such as *Six Feet Under* (2001-05) or *Dead Like Me* (2003-04).

The Addams Family is an interesting case where the uncanny is used for comic effect. On the one hand, this highly unconventional family can be viewed as a parody of the old aristocratic dynasties, eccentric, sophisticated in their own way, but also decadent and disconnected from reality. Nevertheless, a more thorough analysis would reveal some elements that contradict this interpretation. First, the Addams may be spooky, but they are *not* dysfunctional; in an uncanny way, they even represent *the* perfect American family. They are united and supportive of one another when confronted with adversity. Second, they seem to share a typically Burkian vision of aesthetics. In the movie *The Addams Family* (Barry Sonnenfeld, 1991), Morticia says to Gomez: "Last night you were unhinged. You were like some desperate, howling demon. You frightened me. Do it again!"

Even in a comedy, the principles on which the Gothic is based still apply: fear has an aesthetic value, and one can wonder why, in Western culture, we are constantly craving for such strong sensations. Who are the Addams? Are they just a decadent dynasty with eccentric and morbid tastes or, on the contrary, could they represent a Gothicized version of a model family? Could it be that, in our society, only a family whose members share this kind of deviant values can remain functional?

Those questions will not find a simple answer any time soon, and this is probably why, in more than two centuries, the Gothic has lost nothing of its appeal. By confronting us with the bizarre, the unconventional and the uncanny, this mode of fiction-making forces us to reconsider what we usually define as normal, or at least look at it from a different angle.

Three Flavors of Gothic

To this already arresting diversity of Gothic themes and forms, we now need to add another dimension, namely the general "flavor" of this type of fictional works. The Gothic novel is often presented as the forerunner of horror fiction. However, a more thoughtful analysis reveals that this kind of novel came in various flavors, and understanding the diversity of the Gothic is key to understanding its cultural influence.

Chapter 2.2: Gothic Fantasy

Walpole's *The Castle of Otranto* launched what we might call the Gothic fantasy genre. In this type of fiction, the supernatural intrudes into everyday life, sometimes violently, sometimes peacefully. If the first response to this intrusion is fright, other emotions can become associated with it, such as awe, fascination, even love. In France, this genre is called *fantastique* and it was initiated by Jacques Cazotte's short story *The Devil in Love* (1772), where a demon falls in love with a human and turns into an attractive woman to seduce him. French Romantic authors of the 19th century developed this tradition; the most noteworthy works are the short stories by Théophile Gautier (for example *The Dead Woman in Love*, 1836) and those by Charles Nodier.

Although Gothic fantasy shares several common features with horror fiction, we also find some important distinctions. In horror, the supernatural is frightening and deadly, while Gothic fantasy plays with a broader spectrum of emotions. In Théophile Gautier's stories such as *La Cafetière* (coffee-pot) or *Omphale,* "fantastical" rhymes with "poetic". Paintings come to life and alluring ladies haunt the narrator's nights; ghosts are both beautiful and sublime. The encounter with the supernatural becomes a spiritual experience. Gérard de Nerval's *Aurélia* (1855) is another fascinating work, difficult to analyze fully, filled with symbolism and mysticism. In this story, dream, reality, fantasy, and madness are intimately intertwined and weave the fabric of a dream-like, uncanny universe.

Fairy tales written in the first half of the 19th century were often suffused with Gothic symbolism, those by the Brothers Grimm and by Hans Christian Andersen being the most famous examples. These authors did not simply collect and publish tales, but used them as a means to address modern philosophical issues. In *The Snow Queen* (1844), for example, the distorted mirror is an allegory for cold logic, and the Snow Queen herself represents science and technology. The description of her palace is revealing:

> The northern-lights shone with such precision that one could tell exactly when they were at their highest or lowest degree of brightness. In the middle of the empty, endless hall of snow, was a frozen lake; it was cracked in a thousand pieces, but each piece was so like the other, that it seemed the work of a cunning artificer. In the middle of this lake sat the Snow Queen when she was at home; and then she said she was sitting in the Mirror of Understanding, and that this was the only one and the best thing in the world.

The supernatural served also as a narrative device to question the values of our society in philosophical literary works. *La Peau de chagrin* (translated *The Magic Skin* or *The Wild Ass's Skin*) (1831) by Honoré de Balzac and *The Picture of Dorian Gray* (1891) by Oscar Wilde share significant similarities. Both Raphael de Valentin and Dorian Gray were idealistic young men seeking for the absolute, only to have their wings broken by the realities of high society. Both novels brilliantly illustrate the corruptive power of cynical hedonism, a power so absolute that even love cannot counteract it. The supernatural intrudes into the narrative by taking the shape of an object that becomes inseparably linked with the fate of the protagonist. From a desperate and penniless student who wants to commit suicide, the "magic skin" (a talisman made of onager's skin) transforms Raphael into one of the most influential men in Paris. His every wish turns into reality; however, with every wish the magic skin shrinks, consuming the vital energy of its owner, until he dies. The picture of Dorian Gray is supposed to have the opposite effect: it grants everlasting youth. Nevertheless, its effect is the same: it corrupts Dorian's soul and eventually causes his demise.

On a deep, philosophical level, *The Magic Skin* and *The Picture of Dorian Gray* belong to the tradition of Faustian literature introduced by Marlowe and enriched by the fecund imagination of Gothic fantasy. In the 20th century, J R R Tolkien continued this tradition in his famous novel *The Lord of the Rings* (1954-55). The One Ring has the same role as the magic skin in Balzac's novel or the picture of Dorian Gray; it is an instrument of temptation and corruption. War is one of the central themes in Tolkien's works, which is not surprising given the first-hand experience the author had with the realities of military conflicts. However, the primary conflict in *The Lord of the Rings* is the inner one: each character is tested, tempted by the Ring, and each one has to win the battle against his own demons. On the battlefield, the evil represented by Sauron can be defeated, but not destroyed; ultimately it self-destructs, victim of its own all-consuming power.

Alongside high fantasy epitomized by *The Lord of the Rings*, another popular fantasy subgenre is sword-and-sorcery pioneered by Robert E Howard in the 1930s. Conan the Barbarian started his epic journey on the pages of *Weird Tales* in 1932 and has, since then, conquered millions of fans all over the world. Probably the most interesting aspect of Howard's series is the shock of cultures. Conan is a barbarian confronted with the civilized world; in other words, he is a Goth (in the original sense of this term – see Chapter 1.1).

Howard and Tolkien took opposite approaches. While the former created an invincible hero, a rebel without a cause, the latter chose to relate the adventures of a humble hobbit, a character with whom the modern reader can easily identify. In *The Hobbit* (1937), Bilbo Baggins is a typical representative of the middle class thrown into a savage, barbaric world that lives by very different rules. Again, the clash of cultures is unavoidable. Conan and Bilbo are the Yin and the Yang of the early 20th-century fantasy; the former brings chaos into a world of order, while the latter brings reason into a world of madness.

Stripped to its core, modern fantasy can be viewed as a heavily Gothicized descendant of fairy tales. Take any story, add a bit of magic to it, as well as a good dose of darkness and terrifying experiences, and you obtain fantasy. Urban fantasy is a good example of this as it blends horror, hard-boiled and, of course, fantasy. This subgenre evolved essentially from vampire stories, the most noteworthy precursor being Anne Rice's *Interview with the Vampire* (see Chapter 2.4). George R R Martin, best known for his novel *A Game of Thrones* (1996, first installment of *A Song of Ice and Fire* series), also ventured in the territory of vampire novels with *Fevre Dream* (1982). The movie *Ghostbusters* (Ivan Reitman, 1984) and its successor *Ghostbusters II* (1989) also influenced the budding urban fantasy genre. In literature, this subgenre was pioneered by Emma Bull with *War for the Oaks* (1987), Charles de Lint with *The Newford series*, in particular *Dreams Underfoot* (1993), and Laurell K Hamilton with *Guilty Pleasures* (1993, first book of *Anita Blake: Vampire Hunter* series).

Television series *Neverwhere* (1996) by Neil Gaiman, adapted into a novel by the author, proved to be influential. Neverwhere is a parallel world that coexists alongside ours, but normally cannot be seen by us. Sometimes, for mysterious reasons, people "fall through the cracks" and become part of this unseen universe. Gaiman uses this as a metaphor for social exclusion; these people are no longer part of civilized society, lose everything they owned, have to live homeless and obey the ruthless rules of the underworld. Yet, as grim as this place originally appears, it is full of adventure and magic, which makes it more appealing for a romantic soul than our safe and predictable technological world.

In the 2000s, urban fantasy became one of the most commercially successful genres in history, partly thanks to books for children and "young adults". Novels for adults were also successful, for example *The Dresden Files* series by Jim Butcher. Paranormal romance, a genre that developed alongside urban fantasy from the 1990s, is equally popular with teenagers and adults. A series of books by Charlaine Harris, *The Southern Vampire Mysteries* (or *The Sookie Stackhouse Novels*), inspired the TV series *True Blood*. Both urban fantasy and paranormal romance have much in common with the Gothic novel, so much so that one can wonder whether these genres are not simply a modernized form of the 18th-century frightening books. The main difference, outside the style and the vocabulary, is the setting; the Gothic novel is set in the past (sometimes distant), while urban fantasy narratives have a contemporary setting. Nevertheless, all the ingredients that ensured the success of the Gothic novel are also present in the 21st-century fantasy: mystery, adventure, romance and, of course, terror.

Another promising genre is alternative history. Two subgenres in particular draw inspiration from the Gothic: steampunk and historical fantasy. Steampunk, as its name indicates, is the romance of the steam era, a blend of Victoriana and SF. Early examples are novels such as *The Anubis Gates* (1983) by Tim Powers and *Infernal Devices* (1987) by K W Jeter (more on steampunk in Chapter 3.6). Historical fantasy narratives are also set in the past (often in the 19th century or the beginning of the 20th century), in a world where magic is possible. *Nights at the Circus* (1984) by Angela Carter and *Jonathan Strange & Mr Norrell* (2004) by Susanna Clarke are among the best novels in this category. Alternative history allows authors to address political issues of today in a different setting, for example, the relationships between social classes, imperialism, xenophobia, ethnic and cultural identity. Moreover, this genre makes it possible to revive the elegant aesthetics of past times, and this aesthetic aspect is particularly appealing to writers and readers.

Chapter 2.3: Gothic Romance

The term "romance" has two distinct meanings. Historically, a romance is a chivalrous tale; nowadays, this word has become synonymous with "love story". The Gothic romance blends those two meanings. Contrary to the Gothic fantasy, this type of novel does not rely on the supernatural to make its effect, although mystery is invariably present. Farah Mendlesohn and Edward James write: "Even from the beginning, readers detected a difference between the fantasy of *The Castle of Otranto* and the rationality of the other most famous 'Gothic', *The Mysteries of Udolpho*" (*A Short History of Fantasy,* 2009).

Ann Radcliffe popularized what is now called the "supernatural explained". In her most famous novels, *The Romance of the Forest* (1791), *The Mysteries of Udolpho* (1794), and *The Italian* (1797), what may at first seem as the intervention of the occult eventually finds a rational explanation. The Radcliffean Gothic narrative relates the adventures of a young heroine confronted with a mystery and chased by a manipulative villain (aristocrat or corrupt clergyman). She is rescued by a chivalrous Prince Charming, who is of course the love of her life (or, vice versa, she saves *him,* for example in *The Romance of the Forest*) and the novel concludes with that traditional happy ending, a marriage.

This simplistic presentation does not give credit to the talent of Radcliffe; the originality of her stories lies not in the plot itself, but in the artistic approach taken by the author. She gave voice to women – not historic figures, not martyrs or saints, but women with whom female readers could identify. The heroine was no longer an idealized object of the male's adoration that had to be rescued from some dungeon; she could now take control of her life.

The success of Radcliffe prefigured an even more impressive and lasting success, the one enjoyed by Jane Austen, the pioneer of romance fiction. With *Northanger Abbey* (written in 1798-99, published in 1818), the latter initiated the evolution of Gothic romance into modern romance. This respectful parody of the Radcliffean novel is interesting for several reasons; on the one hand, it illustrates the degree of popularity this type of novel had among young and educated middle-class readers; on the other hand, it shows the influence this kind of literature exerted on Austen herself.

The Gothic romance also had a significant influence on the budding Romantic Movement. Several authors who launched this movement not only read and appreciated Radcliffe, but started their career by writing narratives that can be categorized as Gothic novels. This was the case of Percy Bysshe Shelley's *Zastrozzi* (1810) and *St. Irvyne* (1811), and Victor Hugo's *Hans of Iceland* (1823).

Lord Byron and Victor Hugo became the standard-bearers of Romanticism in Great Britain and France, respectively. Byron created the archetype of a dark, hypersensitive, yet irresistibly charismatic hero (or antihero) combining the characteristics of a traditional Prince Charming with those of a Gothic villain. Byronic heroes came in all shapes and sizes: Childe Harold (in *Childe Harold's Pilgrimage,* 1812-18), *The Giaour* (1813), *The Corsair* (1814), *Manfred* (1817), and *Don Juan* (1819-24).

Romanticism celebrated passion in all its forms, even the darkest ones. In this sense, this movement was even more Gothic than the Gothic novel itself. While the latter was suffused with a sense of morality, and was from this point of view a product of Protestant Puritanism, Romanticism breached the barriers between Good and Evil as these notions were traditionally understood. From now on, there was no clear separation between "heroes" and "villains"; protagonists had the right to their dark side, and stories did not have to conclude with a happy ending. Tragedy was again on the rise, and it brought literature to new heights.

Victor Hugo is best known for his masterpiece *Les Misérables* (1862); however, *The Hunchback of Notre Dame* (1831), a historical fiction set in 15th-century Paris, was equally influential. This is a quintessential Gothic Romantic work, yet it is seldom mentioned as such in textbooks.

Apparently, it has all the characteristics of a Gothic novel: a medieval setting, a priest who falls in love with a woman and tries to kidnap her, a handsome and brave young man who rescues her, and, most importantly, the crucial role of the Gothic architecture. But something has changed compared with the 18th-century terrifying novels, and all the clichés created by those are progressively shattered. The handsome young man (Phoebus) loses his status of romantic hero to the benefit of the ugly Quasimodo. Hugo introduces a motif that will become an intricate part of the Gothic culture, the one of the beauty and the beast. This subversion of the traditional Radcliffean love story is an important evolution consistent with the Gothic aesthetics; the beauty is in the eye of the beholder, not in the object itself. This theme will find its most recognizable expression in *The Phantom of the Opera* (1910) by Gaston Leroux and the movie *Beauty and the Beast* (1946) by Jean Cocteau.

The Victorian novel took up the torch from the earlier Romantic literature, retaining its sensitivity while adding a more realistic, social aspect. Famous names such as Charles Dickens, Mark Twain and the sisters Brontë immediately spring to mind. Emily Brontë's *Wuthering Heights* and Charlotte Brontë's *Jane Eyre,* both published in 1847, became part of the Gothic culture, although they have little in common with the literature of terror. The motif of the beauty and the beast takes a new shape with the tragic love story between Catherine and Heathcliff in *Wuthering Heights*. The latter epitomizes the Byronic hero: he is charismatic, but also cold, manipulative, has a troubled mind and even sadistic tendencies.

Nathaniel Hawthorne and Herman Melville are sometimes mentioned in literary criticism as typical dark Romantic authors. Stylistically, *Moby-Dick* (1851) is a lightly Gothicized tale, and its connection to the Gothic is mainly due to the theme of obsession and revenge. Ahab, with his fixation on his animal Nemesis, reminds us of Dr Frankenstein who chased his creation to the edges of the world. Nathaniel Hawthorne drew more heavily on the Gothic tradition. His short stories, for example, *The Birth-Mark, Rappaccini's Daughter,* and *Feathertop,* are typical of dark Romanticism and have much in common with those by Théophile Gautier and Edgar Poe. *The House of the Seven Gables* (1851) is probably Hawthorne's most "Gothic" novel as it features an ancestral crime and a curse. The seemingly supernatural elements of its plot eventually find a rational explanation, so this novel belongs to the tradition of the "supernatural explained", started by Radcliffe.

Wilkie Collins was another champion of Gothization. In his short stories, he creates an atmosphere of terror by maintaining a constant uncertainty around the nature of the events he describes; is there intervention of the supernatural, or is it a hallucination, a dream? He subverts the "supernatural explained" by challenging the realistic explanations and suggesting that there is indeed something unfathomable going on. *The Woman in White* (1860) is his most well-known novel. Other famous post-romantic authors such as Guy de Maupassant also cultivated this doubt about the reality of perceived events. "Am I insane?" repeats the narrator in the eponymous short story, driven mad – literally – by his desire for a woman who grew tired of him.

The Radcliffean model, the one that blended terror and romance, the supernatural and the realistic, was by the end of the 19th century subverted to serve a new purpose: the exploration of the secrets of the human mind. The psychological Gothic predated psychoanalysis by a century and informed Freud's theories. When these theories became widely known, in turn they started to inspire writers and artists. This subject is too vast to be tackled in this book, so I will take just one example: the emergence of Modernism.

Paradoxically, the Modernist Movement, whose purpose was to break with artistic traditions, owes much to the Gothic. Edgar Poe and Baudelaire transformed poetry by making poems more concise and by using less antiquated language. Their goal in doing so was to achieve the greatest emotional effect and conjure up the sublime. Authors like Wilkie Collins, Sheridan Le Fanu and Maupassant aimed again at creating tension by subverting both realism and the "supernatural explained", transforming it into what we might call the "natural unexplained". By doing so, they opened the door on a hidden dimension of reality, a universe unknown, yet familiar, in other words *uncanny.*

Franz Kafka is seldom mentioned by literary critics as one of the greatest authors influenced by the Gothic. I believe this is a serious oversight, as his works epitomize this "natural unexplained" that evolved from the Radcliffean "supernatural explained". In *Kafka, Gothic and Fairytale* (2003), Patrick Bridgwater states: "Far from being a reason for excluding him [Kafka] from the Gothic context and pantheon, the fact that Kafka is one of the jewels in the crown of high modernism is all the more reason for placing him in it, for modernism with its sub-version of existing forms goes back precisely to the period of high Gothic at the end of the eighteenth century."

To conclude this brief overview of the "realistic" Gothic tradition started by Radcliffe, let's mention its influence on 20th-century crime fiction. We already touched on the origins of hard-boiled fiction and the role of Fritz Lang in the emergence of film noir; however, the most famous film director inspired by the Gothic was Alfred Hitchcock. Two films in particular are usually mentioned as jewels in the crown of the cinematic Gothic: *Rebecca* (1940), the adaptation of Daphne du Maurier's novel, and *Psycho* (1960), adapted from Robert Bloch's work. Both narratives masterfully play with uncertainties, and both are psychoanalytic, as the dysfunctional male-female relationships they depict are the result of a dysfunctional psyche.

A good example of present-day Gothic romance would be the TV series *Murdoch Mysteries* (2008-present). The series is set in Victorian Toronto (starting in 1895 for the first season) and revolves around the romantic relationship between Detective William Murdoch and the coroner Dr Julia Ogden. Several episodes from this series illustrate the "supernatural explained" (for example *The Ghost of Queen's Park*, Season 6, Episode 7). When confronted with mysterious events, Constable Crabtree, Murdoch's assistant, often presents theories involving the supernatural; however, every time Murdoch proves that those events have a rational, scientific explanation. Several elements place this series within the Gothic tradition, including the setting, the atmosphere, the theme of women's emancipation embodied by Dr Ogden and her protégé, Dr Grace, as well as a somewhat playful attitude toward death.

Chapter 2.4: Gothic Horror

Horror fiction is a modern form of tragedy. Even to a greater extent than fear, it is the sense of powerlessness that pervades this type of narratives. Horror fiction is born out of the feeling that the world is hostile to us by its very nature. We cannot find happiness, as there is *something* malevolent out there that will pursue us, get to us, destroy everything we care about. This is a crucial difference between fantasy and horror: in the latter, victory is impossible, and even if some of the characters manage to survive at the end of the story, Evil remains the dominant force.

Again, it is Burke who provided the intellectual foundation for what will become known as the horror genre. In Part I, Section VI of his essay on aesthetics he wrote: "The ideas of *pain, sickness,* and *death,* fill the mind with strong emotions of horror; but *life* and *health,* though they put us in a capacity of being affected with pleasure, make no such impression by the simple enjoyment. The passions therefore which are conversant about the preservation of the individual turn chiefly on *pain* and *danger,* and they are the most powerful of all the passions."

Gothic writers drew inspiration from this idea, starting with Walpole. Self-preservation is one of the basic and most powerful instincts and, when confronted with a menace before which they are defenseless, characters have no other choice than to run for their lives. The novel that launched horror fiction, however, was not *The Castle of Otranto,* but *The Monk* (1796) by Matthew Gregory Lewis. In her essay *On the Supernatural in Poetry* (1826), Radcliffe made the subtle, but important distinction between *terror* and *horror:* terror is the *expectation,* while horror is the *realization* that something horrific actually happened or is happening.

Horror narratives can be told from the point of view of the victim or the killer; in the latter case, the criminal becomes himself a victim. *The Monk* relates a fantastical story of a priest tempted and corrupted by a supernatural creature who took human form. Some similarities with Cazotte's *The Devil in Love* are obvious, but the other important source of inspiration of this novel is to be found elsewhere, namely, in the controversial writings by Marquis de Sade. It was Lewis who brought sadism into the Gothic, and we have to live with this legacy, whether we like it or not. Contrary to most terrifying novels published in the second half of the 18th century, *The Monk* was *not* written in accordance with Burkian aesthetics. This novel contains gore in its most graphic and explicit form, while Burke condemned such displays.

One of the first masters of horror fiction was the German Romantic E T A Hoffmann. His novel *The Devil's Elixir* (1815) was inspired by *The*

Monk, but despite the similarities, Hoffmann's narrative gives us a glimpse of the metaphysical dimension the Gothic will later acquire. One of the recurrent concerns that appears in his stories is duality, and this motif will later become an intricate part of speculative fiction. Other themes around which Gothic horror revolves are persecution, obsession, and revenge. In *The Sandman* (1816), Hoffmann expressed the very essence of this genre:

> "Coppelius is an evil, hostile principle; he can produce terrible effects, like a diabolical power that has come invisibly into life; but only then, when you will not banish him from your mind and thoughts. So long as you believe in him he really exists, and exerts his influence; only your belief is his power."

Coppelius is the Sandman, a bogeyman who frightened Nathaniel when he was a child. The latter believes this devilish man to be responsible for his father's death. Coppelius relentlessly pursues him, appearing under different names every time Nathaniel thinks he has found safety. A similar fixation animates Mary Shelley's characters in *Frankenstein.* Victor rejects and abandons his creation, his unnatural child, who exerts a terrible vengeance and kills everyone the scientist cares about. In turn, when Victor has no other reasons to live other than revenge, he tracks the creature to the edges of the world intending to destroy it.

In Edgar Poe's story *The Black Cat* (1843), it is the cat that haunts the narrator and exerts revenge on him (does this animal possess supernatural powers, does it have several lives?). Revenge is again the central theme in *The Cask of Amontillado* (1846) and other Poe's stories. Sometimes, morbid obsession leads logically to murder, but in other cases its effect is opposite: it brings the dead back to life, for example in *Ligeia* (1838) and, more ambiguously, in *Morella* (1835).

During the 19th century, the fear of death was replaced by an even more powerful source of terror: the fear of mental disintegration. This trend, started with Hoffmann, found its most recognizable expression with Poe and continued to develop by merging with the theme of reversed evolution. Darwinian theories had a considerable impact on the Gothic; for the first time in history, people realized that human beings can – at least theoretically – return to a more primitive state. This is the central idea underpinning novels such as Stevenson's *Strange Case of Dr Jekyll and Mr Hyde* (1886), *The Time Machine* (1895), and *The Island of Doctor Moreau* (1896) by H G Wells.

H P Lovecraft's artistic approach was similar to the one adopted by Hoffmann and Poe. He used Gothic literary devices to create an atmosphere dark, unsettling, nightmarish. What Lovecraft brought to speculative fiction is the concept of world building. Lovecraft did not only create a myth; he created an entire fictional world to illustrate his cosmological views. This is how he summarized his vision of our future in the introductory paragraph from *The Call of Cthulhu* (1926):

> The most merciful thing in the world, I think, is the inability of the human mind to correlate all its contents. We live on a placid island of ignorance in the midst of black seas of infinity, and it was not meant that we should voyage far. The sciences, each straining in its own direction, have hitherto harmed us little; but some day the piecing together of dissociated knowledge will open up such terrifying vistas of reality, and of our frightful position therein, that we shall either go mad from the revelation or flee from the deadly light into the peace and safety of a new dark age.

Knowledge is the ultimate destroyer of civilizations – here is an interesting way of subverting the ideals of enlightenment! Never was the human so lonely and powerless, his feeble mind crushed under the weight of the universe and its dark secrets. Suffering acquires a truly cosmic scale.

Any overview of Gothic horror would be incomplete without mention of horror film. Cinema loves monsters, and there is little point in insisting again on the impact made by cinematic adaptations of 19th-century classics such as *Frankenstein* or *Dracula* (the latter is further discussed in Chapter 2.6). In addition to the Hollywoodian masterpieces already mentioned in the previous chapters, noteworthy films were also produced in Britain by Hammer Film Productions and, in the United States, by Roger Corman, known for his adaptations of Poe's short stories, and by Jacques Tourneur (*Cat People*, 1942, *Night of the Demon*, 1957).

One idea in particular that has been obsessing Western society found an original expression in speculative fiction: the fear of invasion. When the exploitation of the so-called developing countries by Western powers reached its peak, the obvious question was: what would happen if technologically advanced aliens decided to colonize Earth? This apprehension caused one of the most peculiar cases of collective hysteria in history. It happened in 1938, when American radio listeners heard the Orson Welles's adaptation of H G Wells's *The War of the Worlds* and believed the events described were real. Thousands of people reacted by calling the police and newspapers, and some even packed their cars and fled their homes before the approaching Martian army, which, of course, was only imaginary. Orson Welles's performance was so realistic that he succeeded in subverting reality itself – a truly "Gothic" achievement!

The postwar period and the atomic weapons race brought new anxieties that added to the old ones. The classic cinematic adaptation of *The War of the Worlds* directed by Byron Haskin (1953) gave voice to the paranoia caused by the Cold War. In a subtler, but even more chilling way, Don Siegel played on this feeling in the *Invasion of the Body Snatchers* (1956). In this fantastical, but horribly "realistic" movie, people are replaced by their copies, sort of depersonalized doppelgangers. This invasion is a metaphor for an extreme form of bureaucratization typical of communist regimes, but it can also be seen as a reflection on the emotional isolation of the individual in urbanized societies. In cities we live among strangers, which sometimes creates the feeling that the urban environment is not favorable to establishing emotional bonds, and, in the long term, solitude can inhibit our sense of empathy.

Horror fiction reached an unprecedented popularity in the 1970s and 80s thanks to writers such as Stephen King, Anne Rice, Peter Straub, and others. Far from Lovecraftian metaphysical preoccupations, present-day horror fiction is rooted in social realities. The most common concerns in Stephen King's novels are related to family relationships, violence and dysfunctional communities. The fear underpinning this type of narrative is not only the one of the disintegration of the self, but the destruction of the very basis of our society. *The Shining* (1977) is probably his most pessimistic novel. The Overlook Hotel functions as a typical Gothic castle: it is isolated, gloomy, and haunted. It is a malevolent place that corrupts the minds of its inhabitants by stimulating their fears and darkest impulses. The traditional values of our civilization are shattered, the family is no longer a building block of society, and relationships between parents and children are beyond dysfunctional: they are homicidal.

Speaking of Gothic horror, the unavoidable question is: what is the difference between Gothic and non-Gothic horror? The major distinction is that the former is never purely sensationalist; fear is a device that allows exploration of the darkest corners of the human mind. Anne Rice's *Interview with the Vampire* (1976) is a brilliant example of this. In this novel, Anne Rice committed the boldest of subversions: she narrated the adventures of a vampiric family, a shocking, yet witty variation on the theme of dysfunctional family relationships. The vampire is no longer just a bloodthirsty, soulless beast, but a being capable of emotion, remorse, even love.

Vampires and Otherness

Vampires have a special place in literature, art, and popular culture. Historically, the myth of vampires resulted from our ancestors' poor understanding of the processes that occur inside a decomposing body. At a certain stage of decomposition, the corpse inflates, creating the illusion that it fed on the living. Beliefs in creatures feeding on human blood are so ancient that it is difficult to determine their origins, and there is historical evidence showing that these beliefs existed in the Middle Ages and during the Renaissance. In 18th-century Europe, cases of mass hysteria where people exhumed corpses to burn them forced the authorities to launch scientific investigations into the existence of vampires. Scientists concluded that the bloodsucking undead were only a product of popular superstition and tomb profanations were outlawed.

In Gothic literature, vampires made their first appearance in *The Monk* before becoming an emblematic character of dark Romanticism. Byron introduced the theme of vampirism in his poem *The Giaour* (1813):

But first, on earth as vampire sent,
Thy corse shall from its tomb be rent:
Then ghastly haunt thy native place,
And suck the blood of all thy race;
There from thy daughter, sister, wife,
At midnight drain the stream of life;
Yet loathe the banquet which perforce
Must feed thy livid living corse:
Thy victims ere they yet expire
Shall know the demon for their sire,
As cursing thee, thou cursing them,
Thy flowers are withered on the stem.

John William Polidori, one of the closest friends of Byron, created the iconic image of the undead aristocrat in his novella *The Vampyre* (1819). Female vampires also haunted 19th-century literature (*The Dead Woman in Love* by Théophile Gautier; *Carmilla, In a Glass Darkly,* by Sheridan Le Fanu). After Bram Stoker's *Dracula* (1897), the vampire became associated with the concept of otherness. Dracula comes from Eastern Europe, and he also comes from the past, which makes him not only alien, but also anachronic. He is a reminder of our medieval past, viewed as dark and violent, and he is also representative of a non-Western culture. The vampire represents *the other,* the heretic, the deviant, the marginal, the immigrant, the homosexual – anyone who belongs to a minority and is perceived as a threat to the established way of life in a given society.

A text key to understanding the evolution of the vampire as a fictional character is *I Am Legend* (1954) by Richard Matheson. I would strongly recommend reading Matheson's book as the film adaptation by Francis Lawrence (2007), despite its qualities, betrays the spirit of the novel. Matheson uses a postapocalyptic setting to portray an extreme case of xenophobia. A pandemic decimates the human population all over the world, and the most horrific aspect of it is that the dead, transformed into vampires, return from their graves to infect the living. Robert Neville manages to survive this apocalypse by barricading himself during the night and, during the day, he hunts and kills the undead. He doesn't even suspect that, meanwhile, his foes are developing their own culture, and that he, Robert Neville, gained in this culture the status of a legend: he became the incarnation of death.

The theme of vampires enjoyed a phenomenal success after the publication of the *Interview with the Vampire*. An important trend in this type of literature is the humanization of the undead; nevertheless, they always remain a source of fear. Particularly popular are narratives in which vampires revealed their existence to the human society, for example *The Southern Vampire Mysteries* by Charlaine Harris and the TV drama inspired by this series, *True Blood*. This kind of fictional universes allow an interesting commentary on xenophobia, racism, religious intolerance, drugs, sexually transmitted diseases and other burning social problems.

The times when vampires were merely a product of superstition are long gone; nowadays, these beings are part of our popular culture. They represent the liminal state between life and death, the past and the present, the normal and the transgressive. They are "the others", the barbarians, the Goths who live at the borders of our "civilized world", who frighten our safety and our way of life; yet they are also our image in the distorting mirror of our collective unconscious. They are projections of our repressed fears and desires.

Other Flavors of Gothic

The three flavors of Gothic described above are not incompatible, and often they do coexist. *Melmoth the Wanderer* (1820) by Charles Maturin is a good example of this, as this novel blends fantasy, horror and romance. Mervyn Peake's *Gormenghast* trilogy (*Titus Groan*, 1946; *Gormenghast*, 1950; *Titus Alone*, 1959) also defies classification. This series can be seen as an allegory, a reflection on the complex relationships between modernity and tradition.

The Gothic comes in all shapes and sizes, but unfortunately we won't be able to discuss all the varieties of this form of fiction-making in the present book. There is, for example, the so-called political Gothic novel initiated by William Godwin's *Caleb Williams* (1794). There is also the Southern Gothic typified by William Faulkner's novels. The postcolonial Gothic is another literary phenomenon we will not be analyzing in this book. However, though we are not discussing those individually, we must recognize their contribution to the Gothic culture.

Chapter 2.5: Women's Rights and Female Gothic

The history of Gothic fiction is intricately linked to the one of the women's rights movement. Mary Wollstonecraft's *A Vindication of the Rights of Woman* was published in 1792, a year after the publication of the first commercially successful novel by Ann Radcliffe, *The Romance of the Forest*. The explosion of the Gothic novel offered women an unprecedented opportunity to express their literary talent and gain critical attention, although the 18th-century frightening novels were quite conservative and did not challenge the patriarchal structure of society. Nevertheless, this mode of fiction-making allowed women to express their experience: social entrapment, disinheritance, persecution, fear of abuse. As Sue Chaplin explains in *Gothic Literature* (York Notes Companions, York Press, 2011, 210-11): "The typical Radcliffean heroine is engaged in a struggle to take back her inheritance from men who seek to misappropriate it, and these legalistic struggles acquire a wider cultural significance in terms of women's struggle for autonomy."

It is no coincidence that a significant proportion of Gothic masterpieces came from female authors: Jane Austen, Mary Shelley, Emily and Charlotte Brontë, and others. Both Catherine Earnshaw in *Wuthering Heights* and Jane Eyre in the eponymous novel are women with strong personalities and not without social ambitions. In the 20th century, abuse (psychological or physical) and injustice to women were also prevalent motifs in female Gothic. The most obvious examples are works by Daphne du Maurier (*Rebecca*, 1938), Shirley Jackson (*The Haunting of Hill House,* 1959), Angela Carter (*The Bloody Chamber,* 1979), and Margaret Atwood (*The Handmaid's Tale,* 1985).

The relationships between the Gothic and the feminist movement have always been ambiguous. One cannot ignore the connection between them (Angela Carter, for example, has been labeled a feminist author); however, the nature of this connection is not unequivocal. The female Gothic is more "feminine" than "feminist"; women's suffering and struggle for freedom are shown by the authors from an emotional, not political or ideological, perspective.

Women in Speculative Fiction

Over the last forty years, though speculative fiction is still dominated by male writers, women made a triumphal entry into the realm of fantasy, notably through children's and young adult literature. In fact, most of the mega-bestsellers of the last twenty years were written by women, and they all owe something to the Gothic tradition.

In Classical and medieval literature, women with magical powers were usually considered an unpredictable, evil force (for example Morgan le Faye in the Arthurian legend). In modern fantasy, this is no longer true; supernatural abilities are used as a device to empower female characters (*Dragonriders of Pern* series by Anne McCaffrey, TV series *Buffy the Vampire Slayer, Anita Blake* series by Laurell K Hamilton, to name just a few). Urban fantasy, probably the most Gothicized subgenre in speculative fiction, deals with themes close to women's hearts, including gender roles. Narratives are often told from the point of view of a female character and the intervention of the supernatural is used as an opportunity to comment on the flaws in our society (for example in *Mercy Thompson* series by Patricia Briggs). Werewolf packs are patriarchal and homophobic, vampires are greedy and hedonistic (should we see here an allusion to consumerism?), and humans are . . . well, insecure, and for that reason intolerant and xenophobic.

Women in Rock and Metal

In music, the Gothic culture offered opportunities to talented female singers and musicians. Rock is usually perceived as an expression of masculinity; it is supposed to be fueled by testosterone. Yet the lead vocalist of the Siouxsie and the Banshees, the pioneer of post-punk, was a woman. Siouxsie Sioux brought to punk music a tinge of sensuality that contrasted with the usual harshness of this genre. In her wake, other talented woman joined or even created their own rock bands: Johnette Napolitano (Concrete Blonde, 1982), Tina Root (Switchblade Symphony, 1989), Jessicka Fodera (Jack Off Jill, 1992), Amy Lee (Evanescence, 1995), Chibi (The Birthday Massacre, 1999); the list can go on and on.

Lisa Gerrard is another singer of legend who left her mark on the history of the Goth movement (although whether she was part of this movement is a matter of debate). The musical project she formed in 1981 with Brendan Perry, Dead Can Dance, brought together rock and traditional music, opening the way to new genres such as the neoclassical darkwave and symphonic metal (see Chapter 3.2). The latter is particularly welcoming to women; the most successful symphonic metal bands owe their popularity to talented female vocalists. Tarja Turunen, Sharon den Adel, Simone Simons, Floor Jansen, and a few others managed to establish a solid reputation in the macho world of metal music. The other subgenre that would not be the same without a touch of the feminine is Gothic metal. It was pioneered by the Norwegian band Theatre of Tragedy and its singer Liv Kristine (see Chapter 3.2 for further discussion).

In conclusion, while consumerism forces women to comply with the aesthetic criteria imposed by mainstream media, the Gothic culture encourages self-expression and gives them an unparalleled degree of artistic freedom. This can explain why this alternative culture is so appealing to creative women.

Chapter 2.6: Gothic Themes and Motifs

Claustrophobia and Fear of Imprisonment

Claustrophobia is one of the most recognizable Gothic motifs. Tombs, crypts, secret passages, confined spaces, prisons, asylums – any places that create a feeling of entrapment or imprisonment are often used in terrifying narratives. Poe is particularly famous for using this device. In *The Fall of the House of Usher* (1839), Roderick buries his twin sister, Madeline, thinking she is dead, yet she returns from the grave. Other short stories also illustrate Poe's fear of being put to the grave alive (*Berenice*, 1935, *The Premature Burial*, 1844), immured (*The Cask of Amontillado*) or imprisoned (*The Pit and the Pendulum*, 1843).

Confined spaces often symbolize social or psychological entrapment. The individual may feel mentally suffocated if society assigned him or her a role incompatible with his or her aspirations. This theme is common in Radcliffean and Victorian Gothic and is sometimes linked to the one of injustice. The fear of being trapped in an unhappy marriage or an unappealing job can also be symbolically represented by gloomy, confined spaces.

Monstrous Space

Distortion of space is a hallmark of Gothic fiction, and this distortion can operate both ways, reducing the space around the characters to create a feeling of claustrophobia or, on the contrary, dilating it. This effect appears already in Romantic painting, for example in Friedrich's *Monk on the Seashore, Hutten's Tomb*, and *The Chasseur in the Forest*, where human figures are dwarfed by the landscape. Human beings are no longer at the center of the universe; there is a sense of humility, but also this combination of fear and awe Burke was writing about (see Chapters 1.3 and 1.4).

Spatial distortion was applied in cinema and graphic novels to achieve stunning effects (see *The Gothic on screen* by Misha Kavka in *The Cambridge Companion to Gothic Fiction,* 2002). This technique started with German Expressionism (see Chapter 1.5) and its bold experimentation with lighting, shadows and camera angles, to find full expression in Hollywoodian classics such as Browning's *Dracula*. The scene where Renfield meets the vampire for the first time is one of the most iconic in this regard. The traveler enters an oversized Gothic castle reminiscent of a ruined cathedral. The master of the house slowly descends the stairs, but always stays at a distance, looking down at his guest. Despite his charm and refined manners, Dracula immediately asserts his domination over the human, and the monstrous castle with its wide empty spaces acts as the projection of the mind of its owner.

Effective use of spatial distortion is also found in fantasy and SF movies. In *The Empire Strikes Back* (1980), Irvin Kershner uses a typically Gothic device to stage the battle between Luke and Darth Vader. The Jedi apprentice faces Vader twice: first in a cave on the planet where Master Yoda took refuge, then again in the Cloud City. The creature he slays in the cave is not Vader, but Luke's evil double, a doppelganger created by the Dark Side of the Force. In both cases, however, Luke is confronting the same enemy: his own fear. This struggle is illustrated by the *mise en scène;* a gloomy and claustrophobic cave in the first case, and a series of sinister, dimly lit corridors in the second. Vader tries to freeze Luke in carbonite (again we find the motif of imprisonment), but

Luke escapes and the duel continues until the opponents find themselves on a narrow bridge suspended over the abyss. Luke's fall into the void symbolizes his defeat, and more importantly the psychological devastation he suffers. Again, this is consistent with the traditional conventions in Gothic fiction since *The Monk*.

Gothic Places

Places often found in Gothic fiction are:

- Castles, abbeys, churches, cathedrals, ruins.
- Graveyards and crypts.
- Old houses, theaters.
- Forests, caves, deserted islands.
- Urban underworld.
- Prisons.
- Secret laboratories and other hidden facilities.
- Ghost ships or spaceships, haunted space stations.
- Decaying old buildings, factories, and so on.

Gothic Monsters

The most typical monsters (in the sense of frightening and dangerous creatures) we find in Gothic fiction are:

- Supernatural creatures such as ghosts, vampires, werewolves and shape shifters.
- Demons, succubae, other agents of the Prince of Darkness, and Satan himself.
- Zombies (in particular in postcolonial Gothic) and de-individualized humans (*Invasion of the Body Snatchers*).
- Artificial monsters: Frankenstein's creature, golems, clones (replicants in *Blade Runner*), androids or artificial intelligences gone bad (*Terminator*).
- Uncanny extraterrestrial life-forms (*Alien series*).

The most haunting Gothic monsters are not the ones we can see, but the ones that live inside our minds. Our inner demons are the ones who corrupt us and can cause our demise. They are a primitive force, an artifact of evolution; yet they are part of who we are. *Strange Case of Dr Jekyll and Mr Hyde* epitomizes the duality of human nature. "God bless me, the man seems hardly human! Something troglodytic, shall we say?" thinks Mr Utterson after his meeting with Mr Hyde. "O my poor old Harry Jekyll, if ever I read Satan's signature upon a face, it is on that of your new friend." The Devil hides in our evolutionary past, and as the development of an individual recapitulates evolution, the sins of our youth continue to haunt us during our adult lives.

The Past Haunting the Present

We already discussed the all-important connection between the Gothic and the historical past in Chapter 1.2. Yet the past does not have to be distant to irrupt in the present with devastating effects. In Gothic fiction, secrets never stay buried, and skeletons in the closets are eventually discovered. No matter how hard Dorian Gray tried to conceal his picture, it is finally discovered by Basil. The same is true regarding passions such as love and hate. In *Wuthering Heights,* no matter how hard Catherine tried to ignore or suppress her feelings for Heathcliff, their romance persists, even after her marriage with Edgar, even beyond her death.

Grief is a common motif in Gothic fiction, sometimes taking the form of obsession. In Poe's short story *Ligeia,* the eponymous woman the narrator loved passed away, and although he married another woman, Rowena, the memory of Ligeia still obsesses him. When his wife dies – maybe because she was suffocated by a dysfunctional marriage, or maybe because she was killed by some supernatural force – Ligeia returns in Rowena's body so they can be together again.

In *Solaris* (1961) by the Polish SF writer Stanislaw Lem, a haunted space station has a role similar to that of a traditional Gothic castle. The protagonist, Kelvin, is visited by a simulacra of his wife, Rheya, who committed suicide because of him. This novel is usually interpreted as a reflection on the difficulties of communication between humans and extraterrestrial life-forms (simulacra are created by a conscious being, the ocean that covers the planet Solaris). However, on a deeper, psychological level, this is a story about the inescapable nature of guilt. We have to live with the ghosts from our past, and any attempt to destroy them is doomed.

Sexuality

There is no such thing as "Gothic sexuality"; each author and artist expresses his or her phantasms, frustrations, and fears. Some authors and artists were quite liberal and "liberated", while others, on the contrary, used the Gothic as a device to express their distaste for sexuality. Lust leads to the corruption of the soul – such is the message in *The Monk*. The fear of rape and sexual relationships outside marriage is a common motif in the Gothic novel.

The Victorian society was hostile to any form of promiscuity. Sexuality – especially homosexuality – was a burning political question. Oscar Wilde was even imprisoned because of his orientation. Some Gothic works from that period reflected this anxiety; for example the novella *Carmilla* by Sheridan Le Fanu features a lesbian vampire. *The Picture of Dorian Gray* alludes to homosexuality, although this aspect of the novel is secondary compared with its philosophical preoccupations.

It was only in the 1960s and 70s that the traditional, rigid view of morality started to give way to a more permissive one. On the one hand, the sexual liberation movement seemed to win the day; on the other, concerns around overpopulation started to crop up, in particular in SF (*Make Room! Make Room!* by Harry Harrison, 1966, *Stand on Zanzibar* by John Brunner, 1969, *The World Inside* by Robert Silverberg, 1971). *Alien* movies shook the world with a shockingly gory version of unwanted pregnancy. In *Alien 3* (David Fincher, 1992), Ripley prefers to kill herself than to give birth to an alien. In *Prometheus* (Ridley Scott, 2012), the archaeologist Charlie Holloway is infected by an extraterrestrial life-form and dies soon afterward, and when his partner Elizabeth Shaw discovers that she is pregnant, she rushes to the infirmary and uses an automated surgery table to extract her "baby". Technically speaking, she performs an abortion.

Confusions between the Gothic culture and sadomasochism are frequent, but unjustified. Overall, sadomasochist practices (and erotica in general) appear in Gothic fiction and art only exceptionally, and they are not always presented in a positive light. *The Bloody Chamber* (1979) by Angela Carter is a subversive retelling of the Blue Beard tale told from the perspective of a young woman who married a sadistic and homicidal aristocrat. Nevertheless, this tale is more a reflection on female self-assertion than a story about masochism.

Politics and Religion

The same can be said of politics and religion: the Gothic as a culture is not associated with any ideology, religious beliefs or practices. The 18th-century terrifying novel was mostly Protestant, sometimes vindictively anti-Catholic. This political orientation disappeared during the following decades and, in the 20th century, the Gothic was adopted by writers and artists of various faiths and cultural backgrounds: Christian, agnostic, neopagan, and others. It is possible, however, that Gothic fiction still bears the imprint of its Protestant origins. Further research is needed to explore this possibility.

Present-day Goths often wear jewelry with crosses and other symbols associated with religion. Nevertheless, it does not mean they are necessarily practicing Christians. The cross is the symbol of eternal life, and reflection on the afterlife was at the very roots of Gothic culture (see Chapter 1.2). I remember the heated debates on the internet about the religious beliefs of some rock and metal bands. When Within Temptation, a Dutch Gothic/symphonic metal band, released their second album *Mother Earth* (2000), some listeners assumed the band was pagan. The next album, *The Silent Force* (2004), struck the fans as Christian. Sharon den Adel, the lead vocalist, explained in an interview to FaceCulture that the Celtic undertones in *Mother Earth* were inspired mainly by the film *Braveheart* (Mel Gibson, 1995). This is just one of the many examples when people see religious messages where there are none.

Drugs, Madness, and Altered States of Consciousness

In the 19th century, drugs inducing altered states of consciousness (ASCs) gained attention from writers and artists. Thomas De Quincey, an English essayist, explored this subject in *Confessions of an English Opium-Eater* (1822) and *Suspiria de Profundis* (1845). Opium was extensively used for medical and for recreational purposes, and its use in Britain was restricted in the 1878 when the Opium Act came into force. Another supposedly hallucinogenic substance that became associated with 19th-century bohemian life is absinthe, the green fairy, a liquor made of anise, fennel and wormwood (*Artemisia absinthium*). The only ingredient of this spirit likely to cause hallucinations is alcohol itself; absinthe can contain up to 75 per cent of it.

The use of ASC-inducing drugs to stimulate imagination was not an invention of rock bands in the 1960s. An interesting essay describing the effects of drugs and alcohol on artistic creativity is *Artificial Paradises* (1860) by Charles Baudelaire. This is how the author presents his project: *On Wine and Hashish, Compared as a Means of Multiplying Individuality*. Paradoxically, some artists considered substances that cause addiction as a means of freeing their minds from the constraints of our material world. For them, a drug-induced psychedelic experience was a voyage, a voyage into the unknown, into the uncharted territories of their hidden creative potential.

ASCs can have other causes than drugs and alcohol, and mental disorder – one of the main motifs of the Gothic – is among those causes. Shakespeare had shown that mental dysfunction can be a source of sublime, and, in the 19th century, dark Romantics drew inspiration from this idea. Literary critics often interpreted short stories by Hoffmann, Poe, Lovecraft, and others from a psychoanalytic perspective. These stories are often told by unreliable narrators whose mental health is questionable. Madness, in particular schizophrenia, can explain the distorted perception of reality characters may have. Obsession, another frequent theme in terrifying narratives, can have the same cause.

Madness is not the absence of logic; it is a subverted mental framework, with its own rules, assumptions and axioms. This is a distorted, monstrous world we can enter and explore at the peril of our own sanity. *The Silence of the Lambs* (1988) by Thomas Harris (movie by Jonathan Demme, 1991), *American Psycho* (1991) by Bret Easton Ellis, and *Exquisite Corpse* (1997) by Poppy Z Brite immerse us in the nightmarish psychological universes of serial killers.

Another cause of ASCs are extreme emotional states. Heightened sensitivity is frequent in Gothic narratives. Several Gothic writers and artists had mood disorders, such as depression and bipolar disorder, that gave a distinctive coloring to their works (Edgar Allan Poe and Ian Curtis, just to give two examples).

I believe that, in the future, ASCs will continue to be one of the driving forces of artistic innovation. Technologically induced ASC is a promising theme in speculative fiction, and the rapid advance in neuroscience is already turning fiction into reality. The human brain is the most complex structure in the known universe, and understanding consciousness is probably the supreme challenge for any civilization.

Part 3: Underground versus Mainstream: Antagonism… or Synergy?

"*Gothic* and *mainstream* are antonyms," some Goths will say. "If it's not underground, it's not Gothic." There is truth to this; however, the Gothic was never totally "mainstream" or totally "underground". This culture is like an iceberg: what the public sees on the surface is a fraction of what actually exists. In the 2000s, the Gothic culture benefited from – or suffered from (depending on your point of view) – an unprecedented period of popularity. Let's summarize the main reasons that contributed to this "outbreak".

Chapter 3.1: Cinema and Television Series

Cinema is one of the most Gothic-friendly art forms. Making a list of all the movies inspired by this culture would be a challenge, even for a connoisseur. A new wave of films cultivating the aesthetics of the dark emerged in the 70s and the 80s, a period that coincided with the birth of the Goth movement. We have already mentioned *Alien* (1979) and *Blade Runner* (1982) directed by Ridley Scott; other influential films were (in chronological order):

- *The Exorcist* (William Friedkin, 1973).
- *The Hunger* (Tony Scott, 1983), a vampire film starring Catherine Deneuve and David Bowie.
- *The Terminator* (James Cameron, 1984), a futuristic version of Frankenstein's monster.
- *Brazil* (Terry Gilliam, 1985), a haunting dystopia permeated with satire and black humor.

- *Angel Heart* (Alan Parker, 1987), a film noir where Robert De Niro plays Lucifer.
- *Batman* (Tim Burton, 1989), a delightfully dark adaptation of the classic comic books featuring the struggle of this vigilante against his archenemy Joker.

Among the most successful supernatural comedies from the 80s, we can mention *Ghostbusters* (Ivan Reitman, 1984), and *Beetlejuice* (Tim Burton, 1988).

In the 90s and early 2000s, supernatural thrillers were particularly in demand: *The Crow* (Alex Proyas, 1994), which has become a cult film for the Goth movement, *Fallen* (Gregory Hoblit, 1998), *The Ninth Gate* (Roman Polanski, 1999), *The Sixth Sense* (M Night Shyamalan, 1999), *The Blair Witch Project* (Daniel Myrick and Eduardo Sánchez, 1999), *The Others* (Alejandro Amenábar, 2001), and so on. *Eyes Wide Shut* (Stanley Kubrick, 1999), a thriller about secret societies, shocked the public with its dark eroticism. Meanwhile, Tim Burton continued his Gothic series with *Ed Wood* (1994), centered on the relationships between this misunderstood filmmaker and Bela Lugosi, and *Sleepy Hollow* (1999). Dark SF has not been left behind: *Dark City* (Alex Proyas, 1998) won several awards, and the next instalments of the *Alien* and *Terminator* franchises enjoyed popular success. In the humorous genre, Barry Sonnenfeld directed *The Addams Family* (1991), *Addams Family Values* (1993), *Men in Black* (1997), *Men in Black II* (2002), and others.

Television had much catching up to do to earn its place in the Gothic culture. However, it stood up to the challenge and breached the gap with its older cousin with series such as *The Twilight Zone* (1959-64 for the original series; first revival 1985–89; second revival 2002–03), *Dark Shadows* (1966-1971), *Tales from the Crypt* (1989-96), *Six Feet Under* (2001-05), *Dead Like Me* (2003-04), *True Blood* (2008-14), *Penny Dreadful* (2014-16), and others. In *The X-Files* (1993-2002), Chris Carter created a dark and sublime atmosphere; the main motif of the series is the impossibility of finding the truth.

Buffy the Vampire Slayer (1997-2003), *Angel* (1999-2004), and other supernatural teen series are also filled with Gothic imagery, although their connection with Gothic culture seems rather superficial to me. Likewise, Abby Sciuto from the popular series *NCIS* is more a caricature than a representative Goth.

The triumphant return of the "might makes right" and "violence solves everything" mind-set in popular culture is an unfortunate development fueled by the post-9/11 mentality. However, not everyone shares this cavalier attitude toward violence. In *Smallville* (2001-11), Clark Kent goes to great lengths to try to save everyone, even his worst enemies (Lex, Davis/Doomsday, Zod). In *Warehouse 13* (2009-14), characters use their wits and knowledge in history rather than brute force to neutralize and safely store dangerous artifacts (magical objects). In *Lost* (2004-10), a group of people stranded on a tropical island try to survive, and they have to make choices that challenge their ethical principles. They learn soon enough that not only does violence not solve their problems, but aggravates them and causes new ones. Maybe we should send our politicians to an uninhabited island and leave them there to survive, just for a few months, so they too can learn this valuable lesson. After that, maybe the world would be a more peaceful place. One can only dream . . .

There is one area of human activity where peace is unlikely to be achieved any time soon; I am speaking of the fight against crime. *Dexter* (2006-13) is a controversial, brilliantly written series that tackles complex ethical issues. Dexter Morgan (played by Michael C Hall) is a serial killer who eliminates other killers. What makes this character outstanding is his honesty toward himself. He is not trying to justify and rationalize his acts; he knows he is a psychologically damaged individual, a "monster".

> "There are few milestones in life that evoke a stronger response than our final act. Death. What was once moving, speaking, killing and threatening becomes nothing but an empty vessel, which is not so different from how I've always felt." (*Dexter*, Season 3 Episode 12, Showtime, 2008)

Dexter's desire to kill is not motivated by some moral principle, but is a result of a pathological compulsion. Taking lives is the only way he knows to fill the emotional void inside him. Yet – and this is the most disturbing part – Dexter is as human, or probably even *more* human than the "normal" people surrounding him. In this series, we also find a reflection on this vicious circle where the victim becomes the victimizer, a common motif in Gothic fiction since *Wuthering Heights*.

Chapter 3.2: Gothic Influences on Metal Music and Alternative Rock

In the 1990s, among all the musical genres influenced by the Gothic, it was metal that embraced it the most wholeheartedly. Gothic metal was originally a blend of death and doom metal characterized by clean vocals, sometimes combined with growls. Three bands were instrumental in the genesis of this style: Theatre of Tragedy (I consider *Aégis,* 1998, as a quintessential Gothic metal album), Anathema (*Alternative 4,* 1998, *Judgement,* 1999), and Paradise Lost (*One Second,* 1997). Other influential bands are The Gathering, Katatonia, My Dying Bride, Type O Negative, and Tristania, joined in the 2000s by Sirenia. Lacuna Coil is sometimes mentioned as a typical Gothic metal band, although their style would be better described as "heavy metal with a female lead singer". H.I.M. (His Infernal Majesty), active since 1991, is the inventor of "love metal" and cultivates the traditions of Gothic romanticism.

Symphonic metal is often confused with its Gothic cousin, which is not surprising considering the similarities between the two. Symphonic metal bands marry rock and metal with traditional or classical music to give an epic, cinematic feel to their compositions. It is difficult to pinpoint the origin of this highly original style; the earliest example I know is the album *Angels Cry* (1993) by Angra that mixes power metal with traditional Spanish and South American music. Swedish band Therion enjoys a solid reputation among connoisseurs; their albums *Theli* (1996), *Vovin* (1998), and others contributed to define the aesthetics of symphonic metal.

Another Scandinavian band, Nightwish, achieved a spectacular breakthrough and imposed itself as one of the most successful metal bands of its generation. Formed in Finland in 1996, it took Europe by storm in the 2000s, opening the way for other talented symphonic metal bands such as Within Temptation and Epica (both Dutch).

Of course, metal and Goth rock are distinct musical genres. Nightwish is *not* a Gothic band in the same sense as Bauhaus. On the other hand, we should not ignore the similarities between these genres, as they are products of the same culture. First, we need to recognize that there is no generic barrier between rock and metal. Indeed, some groups cross this permeable frontier in one direction or another; Lacri-mosa, originally a Goth band, was seduced by metal, while Anathema, Katatonia, and Within Temptation (initially doom bands) are now flirt-ing with alternative rock. Second, let's remind ourselves that the Gothic is *not* a genre, but an aesthetic, a particular approach to artistic creation. Therefore, there is no reason it could not manifest itself in *any* musical genre, from neoclassical to metal.

Finally, let's state that the Gothic is not just a label you stick on a product – CD, book, clothing – so you can sell it to the intended audi-ence. Our goal here is not to define whether such or such band is Gothic, but to understand the influence of the Gothic tradition on present-day music. Even a superficial analysis of lyrics, album covers and videos released by Nightwish would reveal an extensive use of Gothic motifs and imagery. In their song "Nemo" (2004), for example, the narrator is searching for her lost past, hoping this quest would reveal her true iden-tity. In this song, the fear of depersonalization is intimately linked with the longing for an ideal. It is not surprising that this theme resonates so strongly with the young people living in the globalized, post-9/11 world; more than ever, we try to fill the void left by the demise of tra-ditional moral values. In the official video (available on YouTube), the band uses Gothic symbols of faith and death (crosses, ravens, skulls) to underline and reinforce the feeling of emotional turmoil. We find in this song the same fear of mental disintegration that haunted dark Romantic authors such as Hoffmann and Poe, the main difference is that, this time, the danger comes not from madness, but from the loss of identity.

"Bring Me to Life" is a plea that became familiar to rock fans since the release of *Fallen* by Evanescence in 2003. This album enjoyed an im-pressive popular success and allowed Evanescence to win several awards, including two prestigious Grammy Awards (Best New Artist and Best Hard Rock Performance in 2003). As the lead vocalist, Amy Lee, has a fondness for Gothic makeup, many fans assumed the band was Gothic. On a deeper, emotional level, it is understandable why they made this connection. The name of the band gives us a clue to what their music is all about; "evanescence" means "vanishing, disappear-ance". Their songs express the same sensitivity we find in some Goth albums (those by Joy Division, for example), as well as in doom/Gothic metal (Anathema, Katatonia, My Dying Bride, Type O Negative) or symphonic metal (Nightwish, Within Temptation, Epica, Krypteria, Xandria). The underlying fears and longings are the same: fear of solitude, fear of emptiness, fear of mental dissolution, longing for an imaginary past or an impossible future.

Evanescence is by no means the only rock band cultivating this sensitivity. Poets of the Fall, founded in Finland in 2003, is another example; their songs combine the energy of rock with clean vocals and sophisticated, poetic lyrics. Other bands such as Porcupine Tree, Lifehouse, Riverside, Blackfield, and others play melodic, sometimes introspective and atmospheric rock.

Post-punk revival also had an undeniable success in the 2000s with groups such as Interpol and The Killers. "Goodnight, Travel Well" from the album *Day & Age* (2008) by The Killers deals with the traditional Gothic theme of the afterlife that goes back to the Graveyard Poets (see Chapter 1.2). We find in this song the same reflection on the transitory nature of human life that put in motion the Gothic in the 18th century.

Historically, industrial rock was closely associated with Goth music, as they developed in parallel and were played in the same venues. Therefore, confusions between industrial and Goth styles are frequent. Nine Inch Nails was particularly popular in the 90s and, in the 2000s, Marilyn Manson gained much media attention because of the deliberately controversial nature of his songs and performances. Although Manson is not more representative of the Gothic culture than Rob Zombie or Alice Cooper, the success of industrial music contributed to the success of the Gothic, and vice versa.

Chapter 3.3: Fashion

Whether we like it or not, the Goth style is now part of mainstream fashion. Fashion designers love the Gothic; it is fancy and anti-conformist, chic and cool at the same time. Several haute couture brands have embraced its aesthetic, for example, Givenchy, Alexander McQueen, Louis Vuitton (Nicolas Ghesquière's collection), and Ann Demeulemeester. Skingraft and Rick Owens offer expensive, but gorgeous Gothic designs. Alexander Wang's collections have a post-punk feel to them. Brands such as Religion clothing, Oak, Kill City, and Black

Scale offer affordable clothing and accessories in the Gothic style. This is how Black Scale defines its vision:

> Through the vessel of fashion & style, Black Scale brings balance to the lie within the truth interpreted by way of graphic art, clothing and accessories inspired by religion, government, identity and death. (source: https://black-scale.com/pages/about-us. Website references correct at time of writing – October 2016.)

Gothic fashion, as the Gothic culture, is boundless in its diversity. It can be minimalistic and practical, or extravagantly weird. Marko Mitanovski's designs have taken fashion to the darkest regions of imagination; if you wear one of *those* outfits, you are sure to attract attention, even at a Goth gathering. On the other end of the spectrum, the Gothic Lolita style underlines cuteness and modesty. This style combines fanciful, colorful clothing with doll-like makeup and playful headgear. Lolita fashion came to Europe and the United States from Japan, where it was popularized by the Visual Kei scene. The heavy metal band X Japan launched this musical movement in the 1980s, its sources of inspiration being punk, glam metal, and Goth rock. This movement is defined by its "visual shock style" and it inspired a wave of innovation and bold experimentation in Japanese fashion.

Since the mid-2000s, Gothic clothing and accessories grew into a sizable market, and brands specializing in alternative styles flourished, in part thanks to the development of online shopping. Alongside specialized clothing brands appeared specialized magazines such as *Gothic Beauty* and *Dark Beauty*. They are a source of inspiration for photographers, artists, fashion designers, and all those who are interested in the Gothic style.

What are the characteristics of this style? Black is often the dominant color, and it goes well with white, red, dark purple, gray and silver jewelry. In fact, the absence of strict rules *is* its main characteristic; creativity and imagination are more important than conventions. If you wish to join one of the global Gothic tribes (see Chapter 3.6), follow the advice given to us by Oscar Wilde: "Be yourself; everyone else is already taken." Another piece of advice: don't overdo it. Your clothing, accessories, and makeup must *reveal* your personality, not hide or disguise it. The Gothic fashion is primarily an art of self-expression.

Chapter 3.4: Games

The first tabletop role-playing game (RPG), *Dungeons & Dragons,* was published in 1974 by Gary Gygax and Dave Arneson. This game presented an original idea: rather than competing, players had to cooperate to achieve victory. A Dungeon Master (Game Master) was not their opponent, but a storyteller and a referee. In the 80s RPGs gained in sophistication and, with some of them, for example *Ars Magica,* the focus shifted from combat to storytelling and character development. Games became more psychological and theatrical, attracting young people who enjoyed this creative side of RPGs. Some of those games had a strong connection with the Gothic culture, the most successful being *Call of Cthulhu* (1988), and *Vampire: The Masquerade* (1991).

In parallel with its tabletop cousin, another form of RPG developed in the 80s: the live action RPG, where participants perform the actions of their characters rather than describing them and throwing dice. This type of game became the focus of an alternative culture on its own. The theatrical aspect of live action RPGs implies that costumes and décors become crucial in creating the right atmosphere. In turn, this requirement forces the organizers and the participants to develop their DIY skills. If at first the task seems daunting to the spoiled consumers we are, some players get a taste for it and start seeing the creation of their own costumes and accessories as a hobby, or even as an act of artistic creation.

The third type of RPG is electronic; we are speaking, of course, of video games. *Colossal Cave Adventure* was developed by William Crowther and Don Woods in 1976-77. In this fantasy game, the player could explore a cave inhabited by supernatural creatures. The interaction with the computer was textual; the player had to type the instructions, for example ">get lamp". After the 1980s, video games often used Gothic settings such as caves, haunted castles or ruined cities, and this trend continues today. *The Elder Scrolls* series and the *Gothic* series are heroic fantasy games that allow the player a considerable degree of freedom. The greatest pleasure in this kind of game is not to just follow the main quest, but to explore the world, meet its inhabitants, develop relationships with various factions by doing missions for them. Massively multiplayer online games offer even more possibilities, as they allow thousands of players to interact and create their communities and cities.

Wolfenstein 3D (1992) and *Doom* (1993) were among the first commercially successful first-person shooter (FPS) video games, and both used Gothic settings (a castle for the former, a place called Hell for the latter). *Duke Nukem 3D* (1996) took all the horror SF clichés and combined them into a gory FPS featuring a typical alpha male driven by a constant overflow of adrenaline and testosterone. This game is full of humorous references to SF, including *Alien* films, *The Terminator*, *Star Wars*, and others. To create suspense, more recent FPSs used not only Gothic settings, but also visual techniques initially developed by the German Expressionist film (see Chapter 1.5). For example, the player sees an oversized shadow of a dangerous creature disappearing around the corner before confronting this creature a few minutes later. *Doom, Quake, Resident Evil, Half-Life, F.E.A.R., Dead Space* and other series all used techniques inspired by Gothic horror movies.

The games mentioned above, though they use settings and visual techniques inspired by the Gothic, are not necessarily representative of this culture. Establishing a meaningful list of Gothic video games is as hazardous as trying to define a list of Gothic movies or music bands. What should be the inclusion criteria for such a list? The simple presence of medieval buildings or nightmarish décors is insufficient; the plot and, more importantly, the atmosphere, the *feel* of the game must be considered. Games the Goths enjoy (in chronological order) include *Castlevania* series (1986-present), *Legacy of Kain* series (1996-2003), *Persona* series (1996-present), *Devil May Cry* series (2001-present), *Vampire: The Masquerade – Bloodlines* (2004), games featuring Batman (in particular *Batman: Arkham Asylum* series, 2009-present), *Dishonored* (2012), and others. Dark fantasy games such as *The Witcher* series (2007-present) and *Dark Souls* (2011) should also be mentioned. The FPS *BioShock* series (2007-present) has an uncanny feel to it; the game is set in the 1960s and the player explores an underwater city built in the 1940s. This city was designed as a utopia, but is now in ruins; it is inhabited by criminals, mad scientists and their monstrous creations. *BioShock* combines many Gothic motifs such as decay, madness, death, and, interestingly, an alternative view of aesthetics.

Chapter 3.5: Digital Art, Internet and Social Media

The development of computer technology is one of the major factors contributing to the success of alternative cultures. Nowadays, one does not need to attend an art school to become an internationally known artist; all is needed is a lot of passion and some degree of computer savviness. Graphic software became commercially available from the early 1990s. Since the invention of internet, anyone with talent and skill can create artwork and share it with the world.

Present-day Gothic artists can be classified in three categories. In the first category we find illustrators with formal training in fine arts such as Victoria Francés, or with no training, such as Gerald Brom, but who use established drawing techniques. The second category is composed of artists who transitioned from traditional fine art to digital art, for example George Grie. The third category includes photographers and photo manipulators who never had any training in fine arts and started directly as digital artists. Websites such as DeviantArt, launched in 2000, attracted thousands of aspiring artists. More than just a website, DeviantArt is an online community where members can display and sell their work, and propose stock photographs to fellow artists.

Since the invention of digital art, models are in high demand. Several models specializing in the Gothic, the macabre or fantasy gained a following thanks to the internet and social media, for example, Lady Amaranth, and La Esmeralda.

Social media were instrumental in the creation of international Gothic "tribes" (see the next chapter). All major platforms such as Facebook, Twitter, YouTube and Google Plus have communities centered on the Gothic and topics related to this culture. Moreover, social media websites created especially for Goths allow thousands of members to keep in touch and organize events and meet-ups. Online forums are also effective tools to build virtual communities as their interactive nature promotes exchanges of information and opinions.

Chapter 3.6: Gothic Subcultures and Global Tribes

Thanks to the internet, it was never easier to join a global community. Few movements benefited from globalization to the same extent as the Gothic, as it spread around the world and took root on every continent from South America to Asia and Australia. Despite marked regional specificities, some subcultures inspired by the Gothic tradition are truly international; these are presented below. Differences between Gothic subcultures are significant in terms of musical preferences, cultural references and fashion. No one should expect to be accepted just because they listen to some band labeled "Gothic" or wear black clothing. For some, being part of a global tribe is a way of life, and one needs to know the specificities of each subculture to appreciate fully what it has to offer. Joining a community is like falling in love; you never know how this experience might affect you. For some, it is a period of personal development, while for others it may be a choice of a lifetime.

Goth Subculture

This subculture developed around the post-punk movement in the early 1980s (see Chapter 1.6). Goths (or Gothic punks) enjoy Gothic rock, darkwave music, death rock, sometimes punk and industrial rock. They are often fond of German Expressionism and black-and-white horror film; Bela Lugosi is a cult figure for this subculture. Many Goths like dark SF and fantasy. To impress them, one should not mention superficial, commercial bestsellers or Hollywoodian blockbusters, but rather thought-provoking books such as *1984* by George Orwell or films such as *Blade Runner*. Contrary to a popular belief, the Goths are not depressive or excessively serious; they do have a sense of humor, although it may be a few shades darker than the one the general public is accustomed to.

Goth fashion integrates some elements from the punk and the glam scene, including extravagant hairstyles, tattoos, and body piercing. Black clothing and sunglasses are popular, as well as leather bracelets and collars with studs or spikes. Foundation is important in Gothic makeup; white powder or other products can be used to create a pale background. Black eyeliner, mascara and eye shadow allow to bring out the eyes against this light background. Dark lipstick and nail polish can give a touch of mystery that adepts of Burkian aesthetics might appreciate.

Romantic Gothic

If you enjoy poetry, Romanticism and Victoriana, this tribe is for you.

Romantic Goths (or dark romantics) are often interested in literature and history with a preference for the Middle Ages and the 19th century. Works by Poe and the sisters Brontë are essential references; true connoisseurs also read French authors such as Victor Hugo, Gustave Flaubert (*Madame Bovary,* 1856), and Baudelaire. Some romantic Goths have a fondness for theater, opera and ballet. Musical preferences include classical and neoclassical, alternative rock, and symphonic metal. Films by Tim Burton are particularly popular with this tribe.

In terms of style and fashion, the romantic branch represents a "softer" side of the Gothic: vintage dresses for women, Victorian outfits for men, elegant jewelry for all. For ladies, corsets and lace skirts go well with fancy chokers and high-heel shoes. Your romantic Gothic makeup should be fairly light; you can use a foundation or powder a shade or two lighter than your skin. Applying pink or reddish blush to your cheeks will give you a healthy, fresh look. Painting dark patterns with a thin face paint can be a good way to unleash your creativity, provided you don't overdo it.

Gentlemen's attire can include a long coat, a waistcoat (silk vests are particularly stylish), a long-sleeve shirt, a Victorian cravat, classic trousers, silver or gold (or gold plated) rings, and, if you want to push it *that* far, a pocket watch and a walking stick. A true 19th-century gentleman would also wear gloves in most circumstances. When greeting a lady, he would gently lift her hand to his lips, but never actually kiss it, unless he wanted to declare his romantic feelings for her. Nowadays this would be considered old-fashioned; nevertheless, please remember that good manners cost you nothing and are an excellent way to set you apart from the crowd.

Vampire Gothic

Books, movies, and TV series about vampires are at the core of this subculture. *Dracula* by Bram Stoker and *The Vampire Chronicles* by Anne Rice are quintessential.

This is a hard-core, provocative version of the Gothic culture. While Goths may be rebellious, "vampires" embrace the darkest facet of Gothic aesthetics. In other words, they like to play with fear and push themselves (and others) out of their comfort zones. This subculture uses symbols that evoke eroticism and death, a paradoxical, yet logical combination considering the history of Gothic horror (see Chapter 2.4). Being extravagant, shocking to an extent, seems not only acceptable, but even desirable for this tribe.

Because of its provocative nature, the public associates this subculture with all excesses and "deviant" behaviors, including promiscuous sexuality, bisexuality, bondage, sadomasochism, self-mutilation, drugs and an unhealthy taste for the morbid. This image is largely exaggerated; again, the Gothic is about aesthetics, not sexual practices (see Chapter 2.6). It is safe to assume that "deviant" practices are not significantly more frequent among "vampires" than in the general population.

Gothic subcultures are not mutually exclusive, of course, and vampires can also be Goths, Gothic romantics, or be interested in other alternative cultures.

Cyperpunk and Cybergoth

The term "cyberpunk" is unfortunate as this subgenre, as well as the subculture that developed around it, owes more to the Goth than the punk movement (see Chapter 2.1). This subculture adopted an aesthetic that we could call "techno-expressionist"; it relies on vivid colors such as "toxic" green or fluorescent blue, extravagant futuristic hairstyles and accessories such as gas masks. Cybergoths are less likely to be interested in classic literature and music (at least compared with the romantic Goths) and they often enjoy manga, Japanese animation films, and electronic dance music.

Steampunk

This is another example of when a popular subgenre of SF gave birth to a new subculture. Steampunk stories are set in a world where technology is powered by steam. Works by Jules Verne and H G Wells are fundamental references and there is also a growing corpus of present-day novels readers can draw inspiration from. This subculture is particularly appealing to those who like to create their costumes and accessories; they are called "makers". For some, designing costumes and gadgets is a way to identify with the characters of steampunk novels and comics, for others it is an opportunity to revive the aesthetics of the Victorian era while adding a technological or fantastical element to it. From a cultural perspective, steampunk is a blend of romantic Gothic and cyberpunk.

Other Subcultures

Trying to establish an exhaustive list of subcultures inspired by the

Gothic would be a pointless endeavor. Global tribes are nothing like religious cults; they are nebulous entities in constant evolution. Their "members" are scattered around the world and there is no single venue, physical or virtual, where they all meet. The absence of any form of centralization implies that the definition of a particular subculture is open to interpretation. Defining "the Gothic" in general is no simple exercise; defining what is a "Gothic subculture" is even more challenging. Grunge, heavy metal, Visual Kei, emo and other movements and alternative styles owe something to the Gothic culture, yet grouping them under one umbrella is risky as, if we do so, the category we call "Gothic" would become so vast that it would lose its meaning. On the other hand, creating rigid, artificial boundaries around this category would be not only difficult, but also illogical. The most fascinating property of the Gothic is its ability to cross boundaries; we can understand it only if we consider it a culturally mobile entity.

Conclusion

In 250 years, the Gothic went through a complex journey, driving artistic innovation, inseminating mainstream culture with new ideas, challenging our aesthetic values and our views on ethics and society. As a mode of fiction-making, it allows us to look at our past to better understand our present and prepare for the future.

To evolve and thrive, the Gothic needs to remain an alternative, underground culture. When authors, filmmakers, artists or music bands become famous, they are tempted to compromise with the tastes of the public to preserve their popularity, and such compromises often lead to conformism, not innovation. Nothing kills creativity as surely as the desire to please at any cost. Does it mean that the relationships between underground and mainstream cultures are necessarily antagonistic? Not at all. Underground movements never exist in isolation; they interact and influence one another, and they also influence and are influenced by the mainstream culture. Cross-cultural dialogue is always mutually beneficial, and it is beneficial to the development of our civilization as a whole.

Epilogue: Many Happy Returns!

In the 21st century, we need the Gothic more than ever. Resurgence of old religious conflicts, nationalism, xenophobia, crime, wars, epidemics, environmental crisis, fear for our future – our civilization is threatened from every direction. More than ever, we are haunted by the ghosts from our past, and this situation is unlikely to change any time soon. Are we doomed, or can we surmount all those challenges?

The Gothic allows us to explore and overcome our fears by transforming them into an aesthetic. Moreover, this culture is always ahead of its time, rooted in the past to better project into the future. What will the Gothic look like in fifty years, in a century, in 250 years? We can see several trends likely to continue in the next decades, the most important ones being globalization and diversification.

Historically, the Gothic culture was born and developed in Western Europe; therefore, this book has focused mainly on the "Western" Gothic. Nevertheless, we need to recognize that, during the 20th century, this culture spread around the world and it is no longer justified to present it as if it were owned by the English-speaking countries. Japan is bringing fresh blood into the Gothic, in particular in comic books, animated films, video games and fashion. *Akira* (Katsuhiro Otomo, 1988) and *Ghost in the Shell* (Mamoru Oshii, 1995) were the forerunners of a new wave of futuristic Gothic that came from the other side of the Pacific, and now writers and artists from other Asian countries are joining this movement. Original and innovative fantasy and SF are written in countries such as China, India, Malaysia, Singapore, and others.

The Caribbean and South America are also progressively asserting themselves as major playgrounds for the Gothic. Magical realism, a genre that emerged in the 1920s as an offshoot of Surrealism, naturally found its place in postcolonial literature. For example, Alejo Carpentier, a Cuban novelist, inspired Gothic writers such as Angela Carter. The African Gothic, on the other hand, is still largely unknown to Western countries; nevertheless, I am convinced it has significant potential.

In Australia and New Zealand, the Gothic seems to be doing well. My own experience left me with the feeling that there is much we (Westerners) can learn from the ancient and diverse cultures of native Australians. The legends of the Dreamtime inspired me as I found there something deep, something that resonates with the writings of French Romantics such as Gautier, Nerval, and Baudelaire, and also with the Greek legends I admire.

As mentioned above, the other trend in the evolution of the Gothic is diversification. Gothic romantics, Goth punks, cybergoths, steam-punks, Gothic Lolitas – the list of subcultures and styles that emerged from the fertile grounds of this artistic tradition is growing each decade, and this trend shows no sign of subsiding. What will be the Gothic tribes of tomorrow?

With new technologies come new challenges, new fears, but also new ways of life. A century ago, space exploration was just an unlikely, fanciful idea; now it is a reality. Robots moved from the realm of science fantasy to the realm of industrial realities. Computers can now fit in our pockets and perform all sorts of services that our grandparents could not dream of. If cybergoths embraced the 21st-century technology, there is no reason their descendants would not embrace new ways of life such as space travel (spacegoths – the new generation!). Culturally, all the elements needed for the emergence of this tribe are already there: music (Space rock), literature (Space Opera), movies (*Star Wars, Alien* series), TV series (I am thinking of the Borg in *Star Trek* series and the Wraith in *Stargate Atlantis*), comic books, games, and so on.

After space exploration, the next frontier is likely to be the explora-tion of human mind. This has been one of the core themes in Gothic fiction since Hoffmann published his famous stories. With the develop-ment of neuroscience, new techniques will be available to us, and this subject holds promise for authors and artists. *Inception* (Christopher No-lan, 2010) is among the best SF films of the present decade; dark, unsettling, and thought-provoking. I have little doubt that this kind of narrative has its place in the modern Gothic, as it not only challenges our perception of reality, but also invites us to reflect on the realities of our unconscious mind. Could we imagine a Gothic tribe developing around this concept? How would it be called, dreamgoth, oneiric Gothic? Whatever: this would be an interesting subculture to dive into.

Last but not least, we are witnessing the birth of a new subculture, the eco-Gothic. This term was coined by the Canadian writer Hilary Cunningham Scharper (*Dream Dresses*, 2009; *Perdita,* 2013). This incipient "black and green" movement represents an emotional response to the destruction of our environment. Unlike the mainstream ecologists who still believe in a political solution to the current environmental crisis, the eco-Goths reflect on what has already been lost: thousands of species extinct, ecosystems destroyed, lakes and seas poisoned. More than just mourning for the lost paradise, the eco-Goths are reviving a spiritual aesthetic that thrived in the early days of Romanticism (Friedrich, Turner), and that takes a new meaning in the context of the present environmental crisis.

As it is always the case with the Gothic, the past, the present and the future are intricately linked. In *The Romance of the Forest* by Radcliffe, wilderness was a source of apprehension and fear; however, as industrialization progressed and claimed new territories, it became obvious that the real threat to human life was the *destruction* of wilderness. Nineteenth-century authors, in particular Henry David Thoreau, warned us about the dangers of consumerism and the resulting over-industrialization.

I would like to conclude with this famous quotation from Thoreau's *Walden* (1854): "I went to the woods because I wished to live deliberately, to front only the essential facts of life, and see if I could not learn what it had to teach, and not, when I came to die, discover that I had not lived." As our civilization continues on the path of progress, for better or for worse, the wilderness – or the memory of it if wilderness disappears from the surface of our planet – may become the ultimate Gothic space, haunting us for millennia.

No one knows what this future holds; however, one thing seems clear: as a living tradition, the Gothic does not belong to history; it is just getting started.

Follow the author on

Facebook:
https://www.facebook.com/Blakemont.Author

Twitter:
https://twitter.com/blakemont_books

Google Plus:
https://plus.google.com/+AJBlakemont

…and the official website
http://blakemont.com

Further Reading

Gothic architecture

Christopher Wilson. *The Gothic Cathedral: The Architecture of the Great Church 1130-1530.* Second edition, Thames & Hudson, 1992.
Phil Baines and Chris Brooks. *The Gothic Revival.* Phaidon Press, 1999.
Michael J Lewis. *The Gothic Revival.* Thames & Hudson, 2002.

Philosophy and aesthetics of terror

Edmund Burke. *A Philosophical Enquiry into the Origin of Our Ideas of the Sublime and Beautiful* (1757).
John Aikin and Anna Laetitia Barbauld. *On the Pleasure Derived from Objects of Terror; with Sir Bertrand, a Fragment* (1773).
Ann Radcliffe. *On the Supernatural in Poetry* (1826).
Sigmund Freud. *Das Unheimliche* (1919).
Stephen King. *Danse Macabre.* Hodder, 1981.

Gothic fiction

David Punter. *The Literature of Terror* (1996), Second edition, 2 vols. Routledge, 2013.
Jerrold E Hogle (ed). *The Cambridge Companion to Gothic Fiction.* Cambridge University Press, 2002.
David Punter and Glennis Byron. *The Gothic.* Blackwell Publishing, 2004.
Sue Chaplin. *Gothic Literature.* York Notes Companions, York Press, 2011.

Romanticism

Mario Praz. *The Romantic Agony* (1933).
Isaiah Berlin, edited by Henry Hardy. *The Roots of Romanticism.* Chatto & Windus, 1999.
Tim Blanning. *The Romantic Revolution.* Weidenfeld & Nicolson, 2010.

Fantasy and science fiction

Farah Mendlesohn and Edward James. *A Short History of Fantasy*. Middlesex University Press, 2009.
Sara Wasson and Emily Alder (ed). *Gothic Science Fiction 1980-2010*. Liverpool University Press, 2011.

Gothic film

James Bell (ed). *Gothic: The Dark Heart of Film*. British Film Institute, 2013.
Barry Forshaw. *British Gothic Cinema*. Palgrave Macmillan, 2013.

Goth subculture

Paul Hodkinson and Fabrice Virgili. *Goth: Identity, Style and Subculture*. Berg 3PL, 2002.
Gavin Baddeley. *Goth: Vamps and Dandies: The Dark Subculture*. Plexus Publishing Ltd, 2010.
Natasha Scharf. *Worldwide Gothic: Chronicle of a Tribe*. Independent Music Press, 2010.
Natasha Scharf. *The Art of Gothic*. Omnibus Press, 2014.

Index

Note: Page numbers for main entries are in **bold**.

absinthe, 80
Addams, Charles
    Addams Family, The, 49
Adel, Sharon den, 73, 79
afterlife, 16, 37, 79, 88
Alaric, 8
alcohol, 80
Alien Sex Fiend (band), 36
altered states of consciousness, 80
alternative history (genre), 55
Amenábar, Alejandro
    Others, The (film), 83
American Revolution, 42
Anathema (band), 86, 87, 88
Andersen, Hans Christian, 51
Angel (TV series), 84
angels, 28
Angra (band), 86
anti-conformism, 3, 48, 73, 89, 99,
    see also individuality
Aphrodite's Child (band), 34
Arcana (band), 38
aristocracy, 1, 11, 13, 21, 44, 49, 56,
    68, 79
Aristotle, 10, 15
Ars Magica (game), 91
artificial intelligence, 48, 76
Asimov, Isaac
    The Caves of Steel, 46
Atwood, Margaret, 71
Austen, Jane, 2, 56, 57, 71
    Northanger Abbey, 2, 40, 48, 56
Australia, 94, 102
Autumn Tears, 38
ballads, 12, 15, 17
Ballard, J G, 35, 46
    Crash, 46
Balzac, Honoré de

Magic Skin, The, 41, 51
Banks, Iain, 46
barbarism, 1, 8, 9, 13, 20, 52, 53, 69
Batcave, The (nightclub), 36
Batman, 5, 46, 83, 93
    Arkham Asylum (video games),
    93
Baudelaire, Charles, 4, 43, 60, 96,
    102
    Artificial Paradises, 80
    Flowers of Evil, The, 4, 41
Bauhaus (band), 5, 36, 37, 86
Beaumont, Elie de, 15
Beckford, William Thomas, 26
    Vathek, 26, 40
Bible, 27
BioShock, 93
Birthday Massacre, The (band), 72
Black Death, 10
Black Scale (brand), 89
Blackfield (music project), 88
Blade (character), 46
Blair Witch Project, The (Daniel
    Myrick and Eduardo Sánchez),
    83
Blair, Robert, 16
Blake, William, 27, 28, 72
Bloch, Robert
    Psycho, 42, 61
Blondel, François
    Cours d'architecture, 18
Bowie, David, 83
Bridgwater, Patrick
    Kafka, Gothic and Fairytale, 60
Briggs, Patricia
    Mercy Thompson series, 72
Britain, 1, 2, 12, 14, 15, 16, 21, 35,
    44, 80, *see also* Gothic: British

Brite, Poppy Z
  Exquisite Corpse, 81
Brom, Gerard, 93
Brontë, Charlotte, 71, 96
  Jane Eyre, 41, 58, 71
Brontë, Emily, 71, 96
  Wuthering Heights, 41, 58, 71,
    77, 85
Brown, Charles Brockden
  Wieland, 40
Browning, Tod
  Dracula (film, 1931), 5, 36, 74
Brunner, John
  Stand on Zanzibar, 46, 78
Buffy the Vampire Slayer, 72, 84
Bull, Emma
  War for the Oaks, 53
Burke, Edmund, 9, *19*, 22, 24, 62,
  63, 74
    Burkian aesthetics, 15, *19*, 21,
      24, 26, 28, 29, 49, 62, 95
Burroughs, William S, 35
Burton, Tim, 96
  Batman (film, 1989), 83
  Beetlejuice, 48, 83
  Ed Wood, 83
  Sleepy Hollow (film, 1999), 83
Butcher, Jim
  Dresden Files, The (series), 54
Byron, George Gordon, Lord, 2,
  22, 27, 41, 57, 68
  Giaour, The, 57, 67
  Manfred, 41, 57
Byron, Glennis
  Gothic, The, 8, 46
Byronic hero, 57, 58
Call of Cthulhu (game), 91
Cameron, James
  Terminator, The, 47, 76, 83, 92
Capone, Al, 47
Carmina Burana, 11
Carpentier, Alejo, 102
Carter, Angela, 71, 102

Bloody Chamber, The, 79
  Nights at the Circus, 55
Castlevania, 93
Castro, Guillén de
  Mocedades del Cid, Las, 12
Catholicism, 1, 14, 79
caves, 22, 75, 91
Cazotte, Jacques
  Devil in Love, The, 50, 62
Celtic culture, 24, 71, 79
cemeteries, 16, 28, 67, 68, 73, *75*
Cervantes, Miguel de
  Don Quixote, 11
Chaplin, Sue
  Gothic Literature, 70
Chateaubriand, François-René de,
  27
    Genius of Christianity, The, 17
Chaucer, Geoffrey
  Canterbury Tales, 18
chiaroscuro, 32
Chibi (musician), 72
chivalry, 9, 11, 12, 55, 56
Christian Death (band), 37
Christianity, 1, 9, 12, 32, 75, 79, *see
  also* Catholicism, Protestantism
cinema. *See* film
Clan of Xymox, 37
Clarke, Susanna
  Jonathan Strange & Mr Norrell,
    55
Classical culture, 9, 13, 71
classical music, 11, 37, 86, 96
  neoclassical, 38, 73, 87, 96
Classicism, 1, 12, 15, 18, 19, 43
claustrophobia, 27, 32, *73*, 74
clergy, 11, 21, 44, 56, 58, *62*
clothing. *See* Gothic: fashion and
  style
Cocteau, Jean
  Beauty and the Beast, 58
Cold War, 34, 66
Coleridge, Samuel Taylor, 27

Collins, Wilkie, 59, 60
    Moonstone, The, 41, 45
    Woman in White, The, 41, 59
Colossal Cave Adventure (William
    Crowther and Don Woods), 91
comic books. *See* graphic novels
computer games. *See* games, video
Concrete Blonde (band), 72
consumerism, 48, 72, 73, 91, 104
Conway, H S, 16
Cooper, Alice, 89
Cooper, Merian C, 5, 45
Corman, Roger, 65
Corneille, Pierre
    Cid, Le, 12
corruption, 29, 44, 51, *52*, 56, *62*,
    66, 76, 78
crime fiction, 45, 47, 60, 85
Crowe, Catherine, 44
Crusades, 1, 10
Crüxshadows, The, 37
Cure, The (band), 35
Curtis, Ian, **35**, 81
cybergoths, 98, 102
cyberpunk, 6, 42, **47**, 98, 99
Daguerre, Louis, 15
Dante Alighieri, 9
    Divine Comedy, 10, 27
Dark Beauty (magazine), 90
Dark Sanctuary (band), 38
Dark Shadows, 6, 33, 84
Dark Souls (video games), 93
Darwin, Charles, 64
Dawley, J Searle
    Frankenstein (film, 1910), 31
De Niro, Robert, 83
Dead Can Dance, 38, 73
Dead Like Me, 6, 49, 84
Dead Space (video games), 92
death, 3, 10, 16, 31, 33, 43, 61, 62,
    63, 64, 67, 69, 73, 75, 77, 85, 87,
    89, 93, 97
    Dance of Death, 10

    metal, 86
    rock, 37, 95
Decadent Movement, 43
Demeulemeester, Ann, 89
Demme, Jonathan
    Silence of the Lambs, The (film),
    81
demons, 3, 13, 28, 49, 50, 52, 68, 76
Deneuve, Catherine, 83
Depeche Mode (band), 35
depression, 81, 95
DeviantArt, 6, 94
Devil. *See* Satan
Devil May Cry, 93
Dexter, 85
Dickens, Charles, 36, 58
digital art, 6, 33, 94
Dishonored (video game), 93
DIY, 91
    maker culture, 98
Doom (video game), 92
doom metal, 86
doppelgangers. *See* doubles
Doré, Gustave, 27, 32
Dostoevsky, Fyodor, 35
doubles, 66, 75, 76, 77
dreams, 13, 18, 27, 50, 59, 102
drugs, 69, **80**, 97
duality, 63, 75, 76
Dublin, 17
Duke Nukem 3D, 92
Dungeons & Dragons (Gary Gygax
    and Dave Arneson), 91
ecology and environmentalism.
    See Gothic: eco-Gothic
Edward VI, 14
Edwardian period, 44
Elder Scrolls, The, 92
electronic music, **34**, 38, 98
Elizabeth I, 13
Ellis, Bret Easton
    American Psycho, 81
emo movement, 99

Encyclopedia of Science Fiction, The, 46

England. *See* Britain

Enlightenment, 13, 18, 65

Epica (band), 86, 88

eroticism, 79, 83, 97

Esmeralda, La (model), 94

Evanescence (band), 72, 87, 88

Expressionism, 4, 28, 29, **31**, 37, 43, 74, 92, 95

F.E.A.R., 92

Facebook, 94

fairy tales, 27, **51**, 53

Faith and the Muse (band), 37

family relationships, 49, 66, 67

fantasy, 13, 24, 29, **50**, 56, 61, 69, 71, 75, 91, 94, 101
    dark, 42, 93, 95
    historical, 55
    urban, 23, 42, 47, **53**, 72

fashion. *See* Gothic: fashion and style

Faulkner, William, 42, 47, 70

feminism, 3, 71, *see also* Gothic: female

Fields of the Nephilim, 37

film, 5, 6, 23, 31, 32, 33, 36, 37, 45, 47, 61, 65, 68, 74, 75, 78, 80, 82, 83, 92, 95, 102, 103
    animated, 48, 98, 101
    noir, 45, 61, 83

Fincher, David
    Alien 3, 78

Finger, Bill, 46

Finland, 86, 88

Flaubert, Gustave, 96

Fleischer, Richard
    Soylent Green, 47

Fodera, Jessicka, 72

Foetus (band), 36

folklore, 13, 17, 45, 73, 86

Fonthill Abbey, 26

France, 8, 12, 16, 18, 42, 50, *see also* Gothic: French

Francés, Victoria, 93

French Academy, 12

French Revolution, 42

Freud, Sigmund, 29, 60, *see also* uncanny, the

Freund, Karl
    The Mummy, 5

Friedkin, William
    Exorcist, The, 82

Friedrich, Caspar David, 27, **28**, 74, 103

Fuseli, Henry, 27

Gaiman, Neil, 54
    Neverwhere, 47, 54

games
    role-playing, 91
    video, 33, **91**, 101

Gathering, The (band), 86

Gaul, 20

Gautier, Théophile, 4, 27, 41, 50, 59, 68, 102

Germany, 32, 43, *see also* Gothic: German

Gerrard, Lisa, 72

Ghesquière, Nicolas, 89

ghosts, 3, 13, 15, 20, 29, 33, 34, 50, 53, 61, 75, 76, 77, 101

Gibson, Mel
    Braveheart, 80

Gibson, William, 6, 47
    Neuromancer, 47

Gilliam, Terry
    Brazil, 83

Givenchy, 89

glam rock, 36, 90, 95

globalization, 87, 90, 94, 99, 101

Godwin, William
    Caleb Williams, 42, 70

Goethe, Johann Wolfgang von
    Faust, 43
    On German Architecture, 17

Sorrows of Young Werther, The, 43

Gogol, Nikolai, 35

Google Plus, 94

Gothic
American, 4, 43, 48, 65
architecture, 1, 9, 17, 21, 25, 27, 58, 74, 75
British, 1, 2, 22, 57, 65
clichés, 21, 48, 58, 84
definition, 3, 8
eco-Gothic, 103
fashion and style, 6, 48, 79, 88, **89**, 94, 95, 96, 101
female, 56, 61, **70**
fiction (history and evolution), 4, 40
French, 4, 27, 43, 50, 57, 96
German, 4, 22, 28, 31, 37, 63, 74, 92, 95
Goth movement, **36**, 48, 72, 82, 83, 95
Gothic (video games), 92
humorous, 2, 3, 33, **48**, 56, 83, 84, 95
Japanese, 7, 90, 101
Lolita (style), 90
magazines, 90
metal, 73, 79, **85**, 88
novel, 2, 13, 16, 18, 21, 22, 26, 40, 42, **44**, 50, 54, 57, 58, 70, 78
political, 16, 25, 70, 79, 85
postcolonial, 70, 76, 102
revival (architecture), 15, 16, 25
rock, 5, **36**, 86, 88, 90, 95
romantic (subculture), 96
Southern, 47, 54, 69, 70
subcultures, 6, 36, 94, 102
urban, 5, 32, **45**, 66, 75, 93
Victorian, 4, 41, 44, **58**, 74
visual codes, 25, 31, 32, 33, 87

Gothic Beauty (magazine), 90

Goths (ancient tribes), 8, 9, 20, 52

Goya, Francisco, 27, 28, 32

Grammy Awards, 88

graphic novel, 5, 33, 46, 74, 83, 98, 101, 103
manga, 98

graves. *See* cemeteries

Graveyard Poets, **16**, 88

graveyards. *See* cemeteries

Gray, Thomas
Elegy Written in a Country Churchyard, 16

Great Depression, 33, 44, 46

Greece, 20

Greek tragedies, 9, 19

Grie, George, 94

grief, 19, 77

Grimm Brothers, 51

H.I.M., 86

Half-Life (video games), 92

Hall, Michael C, 85

hallucinations, 59, 80

Hamilton, Laurell K
Anita Blake series, 53

Hammer Film Productions, 65

Hammett, Dashiell
Maltese Falcon, The, 45

hard-boiled (genre), 45, 53, 60

Harris, Charlaine
Southern Vampire Mysteries, The, 54, 69

Harris, Thomas
Silence of the Lambs, The, 81

Harrison, Harry
Make Room! Make Room!, 46, 47, 78

Haskin, Byron
War of the Worlds, The (film, 1953), 65

haunted places, 1, 14, 21, 22, 29, 31, 50, 61, 66, 68, 75, 77, 91

Hawthorne, Nathaniel, 4, 41, 58

House of the Seven Gables, The, 59

hedonism, 51, 72

Hellblazer, 46

Hellboy, 46

Henry VII, 17

Henry VIII, 14

Hesse, Hermann, 35

Hitchcock, Alfred, 61

Hitler, Adolf, 33

Hoblit, Gregory
  Fallen (film), 83

Hoffmann, E T A, 4, 22, 41, **63**, 64, 80, 87, 103
  Devil's Elixir, The, 63
  Sandman, The, 63

Homer, 9, 19
  Iliad, 9
  Odyssey, 9

homosexuality, 68, 72, 78

horror fiction, 3, 23, 41, 43, 50, 53, **61**, 69, 92, 95, 97

Howard, Robert E, 52
  Conan the Barbarian, 52

Hugo, Victor, 57, 96
  Hunchback of Notre Dame, The, 41, 57

humor. *See* Gothic: humorous

Huns, 20

Huppertz, Gottfried, 37

Hurd, Richard
  Letters on Chivalry and Romance, 17

hysteria, 65, 67

identity, 55, 87, 89
  national, 16

immigration, 47, 68

imperialism, 45, 55

individuality, 48, 74, 76, 90
  de-individualization, 66, 76, 87

Industrial Revolution, 42

industrial rock, 88, 95

industrialism, 33, 42, 102, 104

injustice, 47, 54, 70, 71, 74

Inkubus Sukkubus, 37

insanity. *See* madness

internet, 6, 79, **93**, 94

Interpol (band), 88

Ireland, 16

Irving, Washington
  Legend of Sleepy Hollow, The, 42

Islam, 10

Italy, 8, 20, 25, *27*

Jack Off Jill, 72

Jack the Ripper, 46

Jackson, Shirley, 71

James, Edward
  Short History of Fantasy, A, 3, 56

James, Henry
  Turn of the Screw, The, 41

Jansen, Floor, 73

Japan, 90, *see also* Gothic: Japanese

Jarre, Jean Michel, 34

Jeter, K W
  Infernal Devices, 55

Jordanes
  Getica, 8

Joy Division (band), 5, **35**, 88

Kafka, Franz, 35, **60**

Kane, Bob, 46

Karloff, Boris, 5

Katatonia (band), 86, 87, 88

Kavka, Misha, 74

Kershner, Irvin
  Empire Strikes Back, The, 75

Kill City (brand), 89

Killers, The (band), 88

King Kong, 5, 45

King, Stephen, 66
  Carrie, 5, 42
  Salem's Lot, 42
  Shining, The, 42, 66

Krypteria, 88

Kubrick, Stanley
  Eyes Wide Shut, 83

Lacrimosa (band), 87
Lacuna Coil, 86
Lady Amaranth, 94
landscape, 24, 25, 29, 74
Lang, Fritz, 33, 37, 45, 61
   Big Heat, The, 45
   Metropolis, 5, **31**, 45, 46
Lawrence, Francis
   I Am Legend (film, 2007), 68
Le Fanu, J Sheridan, 41, 60
   Carmilla, 68, 78
Lee, Amy, 72, 88
Legacy of Kain (video games), 93
Lem, Stanislaw
   Solaris, 77
Leroux, Gaston
   Phantom of the Opera, The, 41,
     58
Lewis, Matthew Gregory, 62
   Monk, The, 40, 62, 67, 75, 78
Lifehouse (band), 88
Lint, Charles de
   Dreams Underfoot, 53
Liv Kristine, 73
London, 1, 25, 26, 36
London After Midnight (band), 37
loneliness, 20, 21, 23, *65*, 66, 88
Lost (TV series), 84
Lovecraft, H P, 35, 41, 45, **64**, 66, 80
   Cthulhu, 41, 45, 64
Lucas, George
   Star Wars (franchise), 6, 92, 103
Lugosi, Bela, 5, 36, 37, 83, 95
Machen, Arthur
   Great God Pan, The, 41, 44
madness, 12, 43, 51, 53, 59, 66, **80**,
   87, 93
magical realism, 102
makeup, 88, 90, 95, 96
Malory, Thomas
   Morte d'Arthur, Le, 18
Manson, Marilyn, 89
Marlowe, Christopher, 12, 52

Doctor Faustus, 13
Martin, George R R, 53
masochism, 19, 79
Matheson, Richard, 68
   I Am Legend, 42, 47, 68
Maturin, Charles
   Melmoth the Wanderer, 40, 69
Maupassant, Guy de, 59, 60
Maurier, Daphne du, 71
   Rebecca, 61
McCaffrey, Anne
   Dragonriders of Pern series, 72
McQueen, Alexander, 89
medieval culture, 1, **9**, 12, 13, 14,
   15, 17, 21, 24, 37, 58, 67, 68, 71,
   92, 96
melancholy, 16, 23, 29
Méliès, Georges
   Haunted Castle, The, 31
Melville, Herman, 4, 58
   Moby-Dick, 59
Mendlesohn, Farah
   Short History of Fantasy, A, 3,
     56
Miéville, China
   City and the City, The, 46
Milton, John, 15
   Paradise Lost, 13, 27
Mitanovski, Marko, 90
Modernism, 43, **60**
Moloch, 32
Murdoch Mysteries, 61
Murnau, F W
   Nosferatu, 5, 31
My Dying Bride, 86, 88
mythology, 9, 10, 13, 24, 45, 64, 67,
   71, 102
Napolitano, Johnette, 72
NCIS (TV series), 84
neoclassical darkwave, 38, 73
Nerval, Gérard de, 50, 102
   Aurélia, 41, 50
New Weird, 42

New Zealand, 102
Nietzsche, Friedrich, 35
nightmares. *See* dreams
Nightwish, 86, 88
Nine Inch Nails, 89
Nodier, Charles, 41, 50
Nolan, Christopher
    Inception, 103
Nox Arcana, 38
Oak (brand), 89
obsession, 59, 63, 64, 65, 77, 81
Orff, Carl, 11
Orwell, George
    1984, 95
Oshii, Mamoru
    Ghost in the Shell, 101
otherness, 68
Otomo, Katsuhiro
    Akira, 101
Ovid, 9
    Metamorphoses, 9
Owens, Rick, 89
painting, **27**, 32, 50, 74, 93
Palace of Westminster, 25
Paradise Lost (band), 86
paranormal, the. *See* supernatural, the
Parker, Alan
    Angel Heart, 83
parody. *See* Gothic: humorous
Peake, Mervyn
    Gormenghast, 42, 69
Penny Dreadful, 6, 84
Percy, Thomas
    Reliques of Ancient English Poetry, 17
Perry, Brendan, 73
persecution, 63, 70
Persona (video games), 93
philosophy, 10, 16, **19**, 48, 51, 64
Pink Floyd, 34
Piranesi, Giovanni Battista, 27, 32

Poe, Edgar Allan, 4, 23, 27, 41, 43, 45, 59, 60, 64, 73, 81, 87, 96
    short stories, 24, 63, 65, 73, 77, 80
poetry, 2, 4, 11, 12, 13, 16, 23, 29, 35, 41, 43, 50, 60, 67, 88, 96
    Churchyard Poets. *See* Graveyard Poets
Poets of the Fall, 88
Polanski, Roman
    Ninth Gate, The, 83
Polidori, John William, 22, 68
    Vampyre, The, 41, 68
Pope, Alexander, 15
Porcupine Tree, 88
post-punk, 3, 5, **35**, 36, 48, 72, 89, 95
    revival, 88
Powers, Tim
    Anubis Gates, The, 55
prisons, 27, 73, 75
Protestantism, 13, 57, 79
    Puritanism, 57
    Reformation, 13, 14
Proyas, Alex
    Crow, The, 83
    Dark City, 84
psychoanalysis, 29, 32, 60, 61, 69, 75, 76, 77, 81, 103
punk movement, 35, 48, 72, 90, 95, 98
Punter, David
    Gothic, The, 8, 46
Quake (video games), 92
Quincey, Thomas de, 80
Radcliffe, Ann, 2, 22, 24, **56**, 57, 59, 60, 70
    Italian, The, 40, 56
    Mysteries of Udolpho, The, 25, 40, 56
    On the Supernatural in Poetry, 62

Radcliffean Gothic, 2, **56**, 58, 59, 60, 70, 74
Romance of the Forest, The, 40, 56, 70, 103
Realism, 43
rebellion, 16, 35, 48, 52, 97
Reeve, Clara
Old English Baron, The, 40
Reign of Terror (France), 42
Reitman, Ivan
Ghostbusters, 53, 83
Religion clothing (brand), 89
Renaissance, 8, 10, **11**, 21, 32, 67
Resident Evil (video games), 92
revenge, 12, 13, 59, 63
Reynolds, G W M
Mysteries of London, The, 45
Rice, Anne, 66, 67
Interview with the Vampire, 5, 42, 53, 67, 97
Richelieu, Cardinal de, 12
Riverside (band), 88
rock and roll, 5, 34
Roman Empire, 8, 20
romance (genre), 3, *55*, 69
paranormal, 54
Romanticism, 2, 13, 28, 42, 43, 50, 57, 63, 74, 96, 102, 103
dark, 4, 22, 40, 42, 45, 59, 67, 80, 87
Rome, 8, 9
Root, Tina, 72
ruins, 14, 15, 16, 28, 74, 75, 91, 93
Rutter, John
Delineations of Fonthill and its Abbey, 26
Sade, Marquis de, 62
sadism, 58, 62, 79
sadomasochism, 78, 97
Sartre, Jean-Paul, 35
Satan, 13, 76, 83
Satanism, 3, 32
Scharper, Hilary, 103

Schedel, Hartmann, 11
Schiller, Friedrich, 43
Schoedsack, Ernest B, 5, 45
science, 43, 51, 61, 64, 67, 81, 103
scientists, 31, 44, 63, 67, 77, 93
science fiction, 4, 6, 35, 46, 47, 48, 55, 75, 77, 78, 84, 92, 95, 98, 101, 103
Scooby-Doo (franchise), 48
Scott, Ridley
Alien (franchise), 6, 76, 78, 82, 92, 103
Blade Runner, 6, 37, 76, 82, 95
Prometheus, 78
Scott, Tony
Hunger, The (film), 83
Scott, Walter, 2
serial killers, 44, 46, 81, 85
sexuality, **77**, 97
Shakespeare, William, 12, 15, 80
Hamlet, 12
Macbeth, 12
Midsummer Night's Dream, A, 12
SHELLEY, MARY, 2, 22, 71
Frankenstein, 2, 22, 31, 41, 47, 59, 63, 76, 83
Shelley, Percy Bysshe, 22, 57
Shyamalan, M Night
Sixth Sense, The, 83
Siegel, Don
Invasion of the Body Snatchers, 66, 76
Silverberg, Robert
World Inside, The, 46, 78
Simons, Simone, 73
Siouxsie and the Banshees (band), 35, 72
Siouxsie Sioux, 35, 72
Sirenia, 86
Sisters of Mercy, The (band), 36
Six Feet Under, 6, 49, 84
Skingraft (brand), 89

Smallville (TV series), 33, 84
social media, 6, 94
Soho (Central London), 36
Sonnenfeld, Barry, 84
    Addams Family, The (film), 49, 84
Spain, 12, 20
Specimen (band), 36
Spenser, Edmund
    The Faerie Queene, 12
St Pancras (train station), 25
Star Trek (franchise), 103
Stargate Atlantis, 103
steampunk, 42, 55, **98**
Stevenson, Robert Louis
    Strange Case of Dr Jekyll and Mr Hyde, 4, 41, 64, 76
Stoker, Bram
    Dracula, 4, 31, 41, 68, 97
Straub, Peter, 66
Strawberry Hill, 1, 17, 18, 25
Sturm und Drang, 43
subconscious, the, 18, 40
sublime, the, 10, **19**, 22, 24, 25, 26, 28, 31, 32, 37, 50, 60, 80, 84
subversion, 3, 32, 58, 59, 60, 65, 67, 79, 81
Sue, Eugène
    Mysteries of Paris, The, 45
suicide, 12, 35, 51, 77
supernatural, the, 3, 12, 13, 16, 26, 27, 37, 42, 50, 51, 55, 59, 62, 63, 71, 76, 77, 83, 84, 91
    explained, **56**, 59, 60, 61
Surrealism, 4, 29, 43, 102
Switchblade Symphony, 72
Symbolism, 4, 29, 43
symphonic metal, 73, 79, **86**, 88, 96
Tales from the Crypt, 6, 33, 84
technology, 31, 33, 34, 43, **47**, 51, 81, 93, 98, 102
television, 6, 33, 49, 54, 61, 69, 72, **84**, 103

theater, **12**, 75, 91, 96
Theatre of Tragedy (band), 73, 86
Therion (band), 86
Thomson, James
    Seasons, The, 16
Thoreau, Henry David, 104
thriller, 23, 42, 83
Tolkien, J R R, 52
    Hobbit, The, 53
    Lord of the Rings, The, 52
Tomb of Dracula (graphic novel), 46
tombs. *See* cemeteries
Tourneur, Jacques, 65
Tristania, 86
troubadours, 11
Troyes, Chrétien de
    Perceval, the Story of the Grail, 9
True Blood, 6, 54, 69, 84
Turner, William, 103
Turunen, Tarja, 73
Twain, Mark, 58
Twilight Zone, The, 6, 33, 84
Twitter, 94
Type O Negative, 86, 88
uncanny, the, 3, 29, 32, 40, 49, 51, 60, 76, 93
unconscious, the, 18, 29, 32, 34, 43, 45, 69, 103
United States, 49, 65, 81, 90, *see also* Gothic: American
urbanization. *See* Gothic: urban
Vampire The Masquerade, 91
Vampire The Masquerade – Bloodlines, 93
vampires, 3, 46, 53, 54, 67, 72, 74, 76, 78, 83
    subculture, 97
Vandals, 20
Vangelis, 34, 37
Verne, Jules, 4, 98
    Carpathian Castle, The, 4, 41
Victorian period, 37, 44, 61, 78, 98
    Victoriana, 55, 96, 97

villains, 21, 22, 44, 56, 57
Virgil, 9
   Aeneid, 9
Visual Kei, 90, 99
Vuitton, Louis, 89
Wachowski Brothers
   Matrix, The, 6, 47
Walpole, Horace, 1, 9, 12, 15, 16,
   17, 18, 22, 23, 27, 50, 62
   Anecdotes of Painting in
     England, 17
   Castle of Otranto, The, 1, 9, 15,
     18, 23, 40, 50, 56, 62
Wang, Alexander, 89
war, 5, 10, 34, 37, 44, 52, 65, 101
Warehouse 13, 84
Webster, John, 12
Wegener, Paul
   Golem, The, 31
Weimar Republic, 33
Weird Tales, 52
Welles, Orson, 65
Wells, H G, 4, 98
   Island of Doctor Moreau, The, 4,
     41, 64
   Time Machine, The, 64
   War of the Worlds, The, 65
werewolves, 72, 76
Westminster Abbey, 17

Whale, James
   Frankenstein (film, 1931), 5
Whig party, 25
Who, The (band), 34
Wiene, Robert
   Cabinet of Dr Caligari, The, 31
   Genuine, 31
Wilde, Oscar, 78, 90
   Picture of Dorian Gray, The, 4,
     41, 51, 77, 78
wilderness, 24, 75, **103**
Witcher, The (video games), 93
Within Temptation, 79, 86, 87, 88
Wolfenstein 3D, 92
Wollstonecraft, Mary
   Vindication of the Rights of
     Woman, A, 70
World War One, 44
World War Two, 5, 37
X Japan (band), 90
Xandria, 88
xenophobia, 47, 55, 68, 69, 72, 101
X-Files, 6, 33, 84
Young, Edward
   Night Thoughts, 16
YouTube, 87, 94
Zombie, Rob, 89
zombies, 76

Printed in Great Britain
by Amazon